ISBN 978-0-266-83436-6
PIBN 10896417

1324

Issued May 6, 1911.

HAWAII AGRICULTURAL EXPERIMENT STATION,

E. V. WILCOX, Special Agent in Charge.

ANNUAL REPORT

OF THE

HAWAII AGRICULTURAL EXPERIMENT STATION

FOR

1910.

UNDER THE SUPERVISION OF

OFFICE OF EXPERIMENT STATIONS,

U. S. DEPARTMENT OF AGRICULTURE.

2

NEW OFFICE AND LIBRARY BUILDING.

1324

Issued May 6, 1911.

HAWAII AGRICULTURAL EXPERIMENT STATION,

E. V. WILCOX, Special Agent in Charge.

ANNUAL REPORT

OF THE

HAWAII AGRICULTURAL EXPERIMENT STATION

FOR

1910.

UNDER THE SUPERVISION OF

OFFICE OF EXPERIMENT STATIONS,

U. S. DEPARTMENT OF AGRICULTURE.

WASHINGTON:

GOVERNMENT PRINTING OFFICE.

1911.

HAWAII AGRICULTURAL EXPERIMENT STATION, HONOLULU.

[Under the supervision of A. C. TRUE, Director of the Office of Experiment Stations, United States Department of Agriculture.]

WALTER H. EVANS, *Chief of Division of Insular Stations, Office of Experiment Stations.*

STATION STAFF.

E. V. WILCOX, *Special Agent in Charge.*
J. EDGAR HIGGINS, *Horticulturist.*
F. G. KRAUSS, *Agronomist.*
W. P. KELLEY, *Chemist.*
D. T. FULLAWAY, *Entomologist.*
ALICE R. THOMPSON, *Assistant Chemist.*
C. J. HUNN, *Assistant Horticulturist.*
V. S. HOLT, *Assistant in Horticulture.*

LETTER OF TRANSMITTAL.

HAWAII AGRICULTURAL EXPERIMENT STATION,
Honolulu, Hawaii, October 25, 1910.

SIR: I have the honor to transmit herewith and to recommend for publication the Annual Report of the Hawaii Agricultural Experiment Station for the fiscal year 1910.

Respectfully,   E. V. WILCOX,
Special Agent in Charge.

Dr. A. C. TRUE,
        Director Office of Experiment Stations, ·
                U. S. Department of Agriculture, Washington, D. C.

Publication recommended.

A. C. TRUE, *Director.*

Publication authorized.

JAMES WILSON, *Secretary of Agriculture.*

CONTENTS.

6 / CONTENTS.

ILLUSTRATIONS.

ANNUAL REPORT OF THE HAWAII AGRICULTURAL EXPERIMENT STATION FOR 1910.

SUMMARY OF INVESTIGATIONS.

By E. V. WILCOX, *Special Agent in Charge.*

BUILDINGS.

During the fiscal year ended June 30, 1910, a new office building (frontispiece) was erected from funds generously supplied by the Territory of Hawaii. The new building is better lighted than the old one; gives room for a more convenient library, and also offices for the special agent in charge, clerical force, entomologist, and agronomist, as well as for a mailing room. The chemical laboratory in the old cement building was inconvenient and has, therefore, been rearranged and new tables have been constructed for analytical and general work. A more efficient hood has also been devised for carrying off the fumes, and a new room arranged for nitrogen determinations.

GROUNDS.

Some of the land nearest Honolulu belonging to the experiment station has been heretofore in an uncultivated and unimproved condition. During the year this land was cleared and planted in Bermuda grass for lawn purposes or in various crops used in experiments. In addition, about 10 acres of land, lying on the slope of the station grounds, at an elevation of about 250 feet, has been thoroughly cleared of shrubby undergrowth and about one-half of it has been planted to cotton and other crops. The chief buildings belonging to the station are erected on grounds which heretofore belonged to the Navy Department and which were temporarily turned over to the use of the Agricultural Department. During the fiscal year this land was definitely transferred to the Department of Agriculture by an agreement reached between the Secretary of the Navy and the Secretary of Agriculture.

DEMONSTRATION FARMS.

It has been felt for some time that on account of the fact that the Territory consists of several islands, located at considerable distances apart, demonstration farms were desirable in order to bring the work of the station more prominently before the inhabitants of the other islands of the group as well as on Oahu. The problem of establishing demonstration farms in Hawaii is somewhat different from that which must be met in the States of the mainland. Farming communities are composed of different races, and a large proportion of the farmers who have small holdings are quite unacquainted with the purposes of demonstration farms. It appears, therefore, inadvisable to carry on such work according to the methods long in vogue on the mainland.

The objections to those methods, in so far as Hawaii is concerned, are chiefly two. Perhaps the more important is the matter of funds, which are at present inadequate to carry on demonstration farms on each of the islands independently of private help. The Territory has freely offered to turn over the necessary land to the station for such experiments, but the Territorial funds available for station use are not adequate for the maintenance of independent demonstration farms. There would be required a large outlay for fencing, buildings, machinery, horses or mules, foremen, and laborers. Such an arrangement would also result in the production of a considerable amount of material which would have to be sold in the open market. An objection has been made to this on the grounds that the station would, in a sense, be competing with practical farmers and with an unfair financial advantage.

The second objection to the mainland program of demonstration farms follows from the nature of the farming population in Hawaii. A community of Portuguese and native farmers can best be persuaded to adopt improved methods, actually shown to be advantageous, when these methods are put in operation upon farms belonging to one of the most progressive farmers in each community. It therefore seems best to establish demonstration farms essentially on the basis of a cooperative experiment. Several such farms will be put in operation during the fall of 1910. The program consists essentially in making an arrangement with one of the best farmers in each community to adopt certain modifications of cultural methods which the station will suggest and to keep careful record of the results of such work for the use of the station and all his fellow farmers. By this method it is believed that the results shown on the demonstration farms will be more readily accepted and will more obviously meet the exact conditions under which the farmer must labor.

COOPERATIVE EXPERIMENTS.

During the time which has been occupied in determining upon a practical method of carrying on demonstration farms, practically the plan outlined above has been put in operation on a number of large estates. The station has undertaken the supervision of certain cultural, soil, and fertilizer experiments on Molokai, Maui, Hawaii, and Oahu. The crops involved in these experiments are pineapples, cotton, rubber, corn, legumes, rice, sorghum, and a number of miscellaneous forage crops. These cooperative experiments have in all cases moved along very smoothly, for the reason that the private individuals concerned were intensely interested in bettering their cultural methods and establishing more extensive areas of cultivated crops, and also, for the reason that a highly intelligent and reliable control was exercised over the management of the experiments and the keeping of records. While cooperative experiments on the mainland and elsewhere, in many instances, cause considerable annoyance to both the station and the private individuals concerned, the cooperative experiments in Hawaii have been strikingly free from such troubles. So long, therefore, as the work can be carried on with relatively little interference with the time and energy of the station staff, it seems highly desirable to continue them where satisfactory arrangements can be made. It is a pleasant duty to acknowledge the active and intelligent interest which has everywhere been shown in the cooperative experiments thus far carried on by the station.

RATIONAL SOIL PROGRAM.

The soils of the Hawaiian Islands are very different in several respects from those which are familiar to farmers and agricultural workers on the mainland. In the first place, the Hawaiian soils contain high percentages of iron in various forms (say from 15 to 30 per cent). In addition to the high iron content, the soils contain more titanium than mainland soils, and in some localities, also a large amount (up to 9 per cent) of manganese. The presence of the large quantity of iron in Hawaiian soils gives them physical properties which are seldom met with in soils on the mainland. Wherever special attention is not given to cultivation, the soils rapidly become impervious to water and air and the iron present in the soil is reduced to the ferrous state. This, as is well known, is injurious to plant growth and is instrumental in preventing adequate aeration of the soil. Moreover, when the iron exists in the ferrous state and the soil can not be aerated, the use of fertilizers gives little or no benefit. It is therefore necessary to adopt a rational soil program, with the central idea that of securing a better aeration and better physical properties of the soil. Studies, which are designed to throw light on the practical methods of accomplishing such a result, are now in progress at the station, and the suggestions, already made by the station chemist, are being put into practice in a number of localities. It may be truthfully said that in many localities the chief soil problems are concerned with the physical rather than the chemical properties of the soil. Improper aeration not only causes the iron to become reduced to the ferrous state, but may also prevent the utilization by the plant of the plant food naturally present in the soils.

The study of cultural and rotation methods for securing a better aeration of the soil will be continued during the coming year, both in pot and field cultures.

RICE.

The chemical work on rice during the fiscal year was concerned chiefly with the study of the time or stage of growth at which fertilizers should be applied and the influence of various elements of plant food upon the composition of the rice plant. It was found during these experiments that the program adopted by the growers, in using fertilizers on rice, was somewhat ill advised, as judged by the physiology of the rice plant. It appears that the rice plant, by the time it is two-thirds grown, has already taken up about four-fifths of the nitrogen and phosphoric acid, and nine-tenths of the potash which will be absorbed during its whole growth; and that, therefore, fertilizers should preferably be applied before planting the rice, or, at any rate, during the very early stages. The value of nitrogen in rice culture has proved in the station experiments to be greater than was previously suspected. On some of the rice soils the use of phosphoric acid and potash gives no beneficial results. On these soils nitrogen alone produces as heavy yields as do complete fertilizers.

It was soon noted in experimenting with fertilizers on rice that nitrate of soda appeared to produce no beneficial effect, while ammonium sulphate was very active in promoting growth and yield of grain. This point has been carefully studied through two crops of rice at the trial grounds, and through several series of pot experiments. In almost every instance nitrate of soda gives no increase of growth over that observed in check plats or check pots; in fact, while it may be too early to conclude positively, the pot experiments thus far carried out indicate that the rice plant can not use nitrogen in the form of nitrate, but only in the form of ammonia. It had already been suspected by other investigators that ammonia was better than nitrate for rice, but it has hitherto never been shown that the rice can not use nitrogen in the form of nitrate.

The importation of rice from Japan continues to increase, and the production of rice in Hawaii has slightly decreased. In order to get further information on the cause of this condition, and to learn more in detail the methods of rice cultivation in Japan and the varieties used in that country, the agronomist visited Japan and China during the past year. It was found that the Japanese have a decided preference for certain varieties of rice which are almost the only kinds exported to Hawaii for use by the Japanese population, and that these varieties are claimed to have certain superior culinary qualities which can not be definitely described. Seed of about 150 varieties of rice was brought back from Japan, including a considerable quantity of seed of four of the best varieties grown in that country. These have been distributed to growers and reports regarding their behavior are expected during the coming year. A test of fertilizers on a commercial scale will be carried out for the purpose of demonstrating the results which have already been obtained at the trial grounds and in pot cultures. It is believed that these demonstrations will lead to a change of method in the application of fertilizers, resulting in greater economy and increased growth.

Experiments are also under way with a number of legumes and other crops, some of which were recently imported from Japan, to be used in rotation with rice in order to maintain the high yield which has hitherto prevailed in Hawaii.

COTTON.

Experiments with cotton were begun by the station three years ago and have yielded striking results in certain localities in which commercial plantings, to the extent of about 500 acres, have been made. During the coming year these plantings will be greatly increased. A number of points have been quite clearly demonstrated during these experiments. It has been shown that cotton will thrive under a wide range of rainfall—from 25 to 100 inches per year—and at a considerable variation of altitude, from sea level to 1,600 feet. The most favorable locations, however, are low-lying lands near the seashore and protected by algaroba, or other windbreaks, from the winds which occur during the winter. Although at elevations below 300 feet a temperature as low as 50° F. is very rare in Hawaii, nevertheless, at such a temperature cotton shows the effect in a marked degree. The leaves even may turn brown, as if they had been frosted. With regard to rainfall, a moderate amount per year is decidedly more favorable for the growth of cotton than a higher or lower rate of precipitation.

One difficulty which has been experienced in growing Sea Island cotton in Hawaii is that of excessive yield, which results in a too prostrate form of growth. In one locality on the windward side of Oahu, where the rainfall is about 70 inches per year, 2 acres of Sea Island cotton required about 5,000 props in order to keep the branches from lying upon the ground and causing the bolls to rot. In this respect the Caravonica cotton is superior to Sea Island, since it invariably has an upright habit of growth. The difficulty experienced with the prostrate habit of the Sea Island can be appreciated from a consideration of the fact that in the 2-acre field just mentioned and in another 1-acre field, on the leeward side of Oahu, the average number of bolls per plant was 700, and on one tree 1,200 bolls were counted at one time. This produces a weight under which the slender branches of the Sea Island can not support themselves in an upright position. An elaborate series of pruning experiments is now under way with the idea of learning a method by which an upright growth can be induced in the Sea Island cotton, at least for the second and subsequent years of the crop. Some promise is already held out by these experiments. A strain of Sea Island, secured from one of the best plantations on James Island, S. C., shows a more upright habit of growth than any other strain of Sea Island which has thus far been secured.

The Caravonica cotton continues to give promising results. During the first year of its growth the yield appears to be normally low, but in the second year a heavy yield is obtained, which, in conjunction with the greater ease of picking and the higher percentage of lint, makes a choice between Sea Island and Caravonica somewhat doubtful. Egyptian cotton has given results as satisfactory as those obtained with Sea Island. The strains of Egyptian cotton with which the station is experimenting grow rather more vigorously than the Sea Island, and the yield is perhaps slightly larger. The place which Egyptian cotton should take in the agriculture of Hawaii will largely be determined by the future demands of the market for the three chief types of cotton now grown in the Territory. In addition to Sea Island, Caravonica, and Egyptian cottons, experiments are being made with Chinese upland, a number of varieties of upland from the Southern States, and a cotton with red lint, from Cuba. It is proposed to make a reciprocal cross between Sea Island and Kidney cottons in order to determine whether Caravonica cotton was originated in this manner and whether an improvement upon the ordinary type of Caravonica can thus be secured. Several plants have been found in different localities in the Territory where a natural cross between a pure Sea Island and a pure Kidney cotton could have taken place, and these plants strikingly resemble, in habit of growth and quality of lint, the ordinary type of Caravonica cotton.

It has been found that pure strains can be propagated by means of cotton cuttings, and a number of cuttings will come into bearing during the present season. In addition to this method of propagation budding has been tried on a large scale. Propagation is an easy matter by the method of budding, but the economy of the method on a commercial scale has not yet been determined. According to the present outlook it seems an economic proposition to bud over large areas with bud wood from the best plants, and thus secure a uniform cotton over the whole field. This method would, of course, have no value except where cotton is cultivated as a perennial crop.

PINEAPPLES.

In connection with the study of manganese in the soil as affecting the growth of pineapples, experiments have been made with a number of crops which could possibly be grown in rotation with pineapples or to replace pineapples in the manganiferous soils. For this purpose corn, rice, and various other cereals, tobacco, cotton, legumes, garden vegetables, and fruit trees were used. It has been found that manganese invariably causes a yellowing of all the leaves and a premature falling of the lower leaves on all plants with which experiments have been made. The plants may subsequently become green, just before the fruiting period, at which time a vigorous growth may be observed for a short period. The ultimate outcome, however, is in all instances a decidedly stunted growth and small yield. The root system in manganiferous soils is peculiar in the length and fineness of the small roots. The ultimate outcome in pot experiments is a root system strikingly different from that in ordinary garden soils. Apparently the extreme fineness of the roots is due to the lack of resistance which they meet in penetrating manganiferous soils. These soils invariably remain loose like ashes, no matter how frequently or heavily they may be irrigated.

In the fertilizer experiments with pineapples, which are being continued by the chemist, it has been found that phosphates, particularly acid and reverted phosphates, have a beneficial effect upon the growth of the pineapple plants, probably for the reason that these materials tend to render the manganiferous salts in the soil less soluble. Lime, on the other hand, is decidedly injurious on manganiferous soils, as shown by the experiments of the station and by tests which have been tried by growers on a commercial scale. The injurious effect of lime is possibly due to the fact that it helps to furnish conditions favorable for the formation of the higher oxids of manganese, which are the most injurious salts of this mineral.

A study of the ripening of pineapples has disclosed the fact that the sugar content of the fruit is derived exclusively from the leaves of the plant and does not increase after the fruit has been removed from the plant. If pineapples are picked green and allowed to ripen the sugar content at complete ripeness is the same as it was when the fruit was removed from the plants. An analysis of the fruit shows that they contain no substance which can be changed into sugar during the ripening process. Fruits picked too green and allowed to ripen, therefore, lack greatly in sugar content and in flavor. The sugar content of green fruits, or fruits ripened after being picked too green, is about 2 or 3 per cent, while that of fruits ripened on the plant ranges from 9 to 15 per cent. The ripening process in fruits picked green appears to consist largely in a softening of the tissues. A microscopic examination of sections of green pineapples shows that the cell walls in the parenchyma of the fruit are greatly thickened, but become extremely thin in ripening. It is obvious from these facts that in order to obtain a good flavor in fresh fruit the fruit should not be picked until the sugar content has become fairly high and the fruits have turned yellow to the extent of about one-fourth their length at the base.

HORTICULTURAL INVESTIGATIONS.

Satisfactory progress has been made in propagating avocados, especially by budding. The method reported in the last annual report has been put into operation on other trees, and the results thus far obtained are very promising. A number of difficulties, particularly the drying of the bud, have been successfully overcome.

Attention has been given to the varieties of avocados to be found in the Territory. There appear to be quite a number of recognizable varieties, but most of them have not been definitely named. Four varieties of special merit have received attention on account of their being especially adapted to shipping, extra late, extra early, or of exceptional quality.

Similarly with mangoes, the methods of propagation reported in the last report and in Bulletin 20 of this station, have continued to give good results. In one case fruit was borne upon a graft within eighteen months after insertion. Continued tests of the possibility of transplanting mango trees have shown that this operation is relatively simple and successful in the majority of cases. The insect pests and fungus diseases of avocados and mangoes have not proved to be especially serious when proper treatments are applied.

A large collection of papaya seed was made from trees in various localities whose fruit was reported to be of special value or of excellent flavor. From the observations made on papayas there seem to be two distinct types (diœcious and monœcious), in Hawaii, with various intermediate forms. The diœcious type occasionally has a fruit borne among the staminate flowers. The monœcious type of papaya bears fruit on every tree. The monœcious type has both perfect and staminate flowers on the same tree and is the one which lends itself best to breeding and selection. As long as the diœcious type is used one must depend upon cross-fertilization, and the characters can not be fixed as readily as where close fertilization can be carried on. Moreover, when the diœcious type is used, a certain percentage of trees will prove to be males, and therefore sterile. A large amount of space in the orchards is thus lost, as well as the time which has been expended in cultivating the male trees. There is considerable evidence that ultimately a strain of papayas will be produced which will come true to seed. Since seed is the only apparent practical means of propagating papayas, it seems wise to make every possible effort to obtain seed with fixed characters.

It was considered desirable to learn the state of the market in San Francisco for sweet potatoes during the season when sweet potatoes are not to be had in that city from local sources. For this purpose two shipments were made from the station, with the result that all varieties, of whatever color, if of standard size, were accepted at 8 cents per pound in San Francisco. The market price of sweet potatoes in Honolulu is usually from 70 cents to $1 per hundred. It would be, therefore, obviously a good practice to make at least one planting of sweet potatoes for the purpose of shipment to California sometime during the interval between the first of May and the middle of July.

ENTOMOLOGICAL INVESTIGATIONS.

During the year the attention of the entomologist was directed to a number of miscellaneous insect outbreaks, to the insects of the sweet potato, and certain enemies of forage crops, and to the propagation of parasites, particularly for the algaroba bean weevil. A bulletin on sweet potato insects has been prepared and will be issued during the coming year. Considerable time has been spent in studying the insect enemies of corn, and it is proposed to take up a study of the chief pests of the principal forage crops in Hawaii as occasion may offer.

More than 2,000 parasites of bean weevils, obtained through the Bureau of Entomology of the United States Department of Agriculture, in mesquite pods, were reared at the station and turned out at various points on Oahu, Maui, and Molokai. The result of this importation of parasites is not yet apparent, but one egg parasite appears to have become quite effective during the past season.

RUBBER.

Opportunity was had during the year to visit all of the commercial rubber plantings of the Territory. These are located on the windward side of Maui and in the Puna district of Hawaii. A satisfactory growth is manifested everywhere in the rubber plantations between the lowest altitudes and an elevation of 1,400 feet. No commercial plantings have been made at higher elevations. On all of the plantations Ceara rubber grows much more rapidly than Hevea rubber. The latter does not make as rapid growth in Hawaii as it is reported to make in the Straits Settlements and Ceylon. The question whether Hevea should be extensively planted in Hawaii seems to depend on whether the ultimate yield will be enough larger than that of Ceara to counterbalance the long waiting period for the first tapping.

Wherever clean cultivation has been adopted, the growth of the trees is incomparably more rapid than where no cultivation has been practiced. Trees which have received clean cultivation since planting are larger at 2 years of age than 6-year-old trees which have not been cultivated. The necessity of cultivation is apparently, for the most part, due to the lack of aeration and the presence of stagnant water in the soil. As soon as cultivation is begun the soils allow the passage of water much more freely and drainage is decidedly better.

Where the rocky nature of the soil will not permit cultivation, it is necessary to destroy the weeds by other means, and a comparative experiment has been made to determine the effectiveness of sulphate of iron and arsenite of soda as herbicides. The cost of spraying with arsenite of soda is a little less than with sulphate of iron, and its effectiveness appears to be greater. About 500 acres of land in the rubber plantations have been sprayed with arsenite of soda. This land is of a rough nature and is covered with both shrubby and herbaceous weeds of a great variety. From one to three applications of arsenite of soda are required to clean the land of all vegetation. Even lantana and other shrubby plants are killed down to the ground by the spray. The total cost for material and labor ranges from $1.25 to $2 per acre; the expense, is, therefore, much less than that incurred by hand or horse implements. Arsenite of soda has also been used at the station on a number of weeds, including Japanese nut grass, which is probably the worst weed in cultivated land in the Territory of Hawaii. This weed is killed down to the ground by a single application of either arsenite of soda or sulphate of iron. It sprouts up again after a considerable interval, but the young plants are weak and may be destroyed by a second application.

TARO.

There are lands in the Territory which are known to have been cultivated almost continuously to taro for several hundred years. The station has made an arrangement to carry on a fertilizer test on a taro plantation which has been continuously in this crop for 200 years. In some fields of the plantation a decided diminution in yield has been noticed. On account of the active interest which the plantation managers take in the matter, this is believed to be a particularly favorable opportunity to learn the fertilizer requirements of taro and to compare them with conditions met in rice culture under water.

BROOM CORN.

A considerable quantity of broom-corn seed was distributed to growers in different parts of the Territory, and about 1 acre was planted on the station grounds. The seed was planted rather late, and the crop was, therefore, attacked by plant lice to a most unusual extent. The growth of uninfested plants was quite satisfactory, and heads of normal size are now forming. If the cultivation of broom corn proves to be a paying line of farming, it is proposed to build a broom factory in Honolulu for the local trade.

REPORT OF THE ENTOMOLOGIST.

By D. T. FULLAWAY.

GENERAL NOTES.

During the year the usual insects were noticed attacking agricultural crops. Some recently introduced pests have increased to an alarming extent and exemplify the destructiveness of harmful insects in the absence of natural enemies. Outbreaks of cutworms and army worms occurred in many localities during the winter, causing severe losses. The rice crop was not affected this year, but several wheat fields were devastated. The corn leaf aphis contributed to the destruction of the wheat and barley crops. In the fall pineapple plants on the Consolidated Pineapple Co.'s plantation were badly damaged by an introduced locustid, *Xiphidium varipenne*. The insect attacked the leaves of the pineapple, making large abrasions which permitted the entrance of fungus hyphæ, causing the leaves to wilt and die back. This feeding habit is very extraordinary for the insect, which usually feeds on pollen. The eggs of the locustid are much parasitized, so that it is not likely to become a serious pest of pineapples. The injury, in fact, has not continued. The edible nuts of the litchi tree in several Honolulu gardens were badly attacked in July by a tortricid moth, *Cryptophlebia illepida*. The larvæ bore into the succulent fruit and render it unfit for use. On the trees of one private orchard practically the entire crop was destroyed. An attempt was made the present year to prevent this loss by spraying, but the crop of nuts was small, and the moth did not appear to be very troublesome, although it was present as usual in klu and koa pods.

Some attention was given to bee keeping, but nothing done in the way of investigation. It is a pleasure to record that this minor industry is now well established here. The bee keepers are progressive, and the industry is growing. One corporation keeping bees has gone extensively into queen rearing, and during the last year several Japanese and Australian apiaries were supplied with queens from these islands. No new bee plants were introduced, but the better of those already secured were rather freely distributed.

Numerous inquiries which were received during the year in regard to insect pests and remedies for them were answered by correspondence. In some cases personal inspection of the conditions was made

19

and advice offered. The station's collection of economic insects was maintained and much material added. New office rooms and much new and better equipment were secured.

While matters of immediate concern received due attention, the work of the entomologist was, as far as possible, confined to definite lines of investigation. This kind of work is believed to be more progressive and permanent than scattered efforts with an immediate object in view.

ALGAROBA WEEVIL PARASITES.

At the beginning of the year shipments of bean weevil parasites were received through the cooperation of the Bureau of Entomology, United States Department of Agriculture, and much time was given to taking care of the material, securing the parasites, and releasing them. Later a search was made to find if they had become established, but this could not be verified except in the case of the minute egg parasite (Trichogramminæ), which bred freely from the eggs of bean weevils on beans brought in from the field. The following is a detailed report of this attempted introduction:

Lot 1 (June). One box of pods of the mesquite, infested with *Bruchus prosopis* and *B. amicus*, from Dr. F. H. Chittenden. Parasites obtained from this lot were all *Heterospilus* sp.

Lot 2 (July). Three boxes of mesquite beans containing *B. prosopis* and *B. amicus*, from Mr. W. D. Hunter. Parasites obtained were *Heterospilus* sp. and *Urosigalphus bruchiphagus*.

Lot 3 (August). One large box containing 30 pounds of mesquite beans with *B. prosopis* and *B. amicus*, from Mr. W. D. Hunter. Parasites obtained were *Heterospilus* sp., *Urosigalphus bruchiphagus*, *Eurytoma tylodermatis*, and Trichogrammid.

Lot 4 (August). Two boxes containing *B. prosopis* and *B. amicus*, from Mr. W. D. Hunter. Parasites obtained principally *Heterospilus* sp.

Lot 5 (September). Two boxes containing *B. prosopis* and *B. amicus*, from Mr. W. D. Hunter. Parasites obtained were *Heterospilus* sp. and *Urosigalphus bruchiphagus*.

Lot 6 (September). One large box containing 30 pounds of mesquite beans with *B. prosopis* and *B. amicus*. Parasites obtained were *Heterospilus* sp., *Urosigalphus bruchiphagus*, *Eurytoma tylodermatis*, *Cerambycobius cushmani*, and Trichogrammid.

All attempts to breed the parasites in confinement failed. The parasite house, which offered the only secure place for breeding work, was too dry and hot. In the breeding house it was necessary to place the material in breeding jars and there the beans molded. Under the circumstances it was necessary to liberate the parasites at once and allow them to take their chances in the field. On advice, only

Heterospilus sp. was released, and in all 2,303 were liberated—a fair proportion being males, with which the females had been confined from five to ten days before liberation. This parasite has not been seen since. The parasites were mostly liberated on the grounds of the experiment station. One lot of 250 specimens was released on the Alexander and Baldwin plantation at Puunene, Maui; another lot of 200 on the Isenberg ranch at Waialae, Oahu; and another lot of 100 on the Molokai ranch near Kaunakakai. Attempts to breed *Eurytoma tylodermatis*, of which probably 50 were obtained, in confinement were unsuccessful.

INSECTS OF FIELD CROPS.

Considerable time was given during the winter to the investigation of the insects affecting field crops. The greatest hindrance to the diversification of agriculture in these islands has been the ravages of insects, and numerous attempts to grow cereals and the ordinary field crops have ended in failure, owing to sudden and severe attacks of insect pests which have been half-heartedly and unsuccessfully coped with. The object of the investigation was to learn what insects attack field crops and their method of attack, in order to suggest means of combating them successfuly. An excellent opportunity was offered to begin this kind of a study in the 200-acre experiment at Kunia, on this island. The locality in which the Kunia Development Co.'s operations are being conducted is typical of much of the land that is available for diversified farming. It was new land, without water, and close to the mountains. All the elements of chance in diversified farming were present. The results of the first year's cultivation suggested plainly that success or nonsuccess depends largely on whether or not effective measures are adopted to suppress insect pests and are applied with thoroughness.

The crops under observation were corn, wheat, barley, oats, jack beans, and cotton.

CORN.

The following insects were observed to attack corn:

Cutworms (*Agrotis ypsilon* and *A. crinigera*).[1]
Army worm (*Cirphis unipuncta*).[1]
Grass army worm (*Spodoptera mauritia*).[1]
Looper (*Plusia chalcites*).
Angoumois grain moth (*Sitotroga cerealella*).[2]
Corn leaf aphis (*Aphis maidis*).[3]
Corn leafhopper (*Peregrinus maidis*).
Rice weevil (*Calandra oryza*).

[1] Hawaiian Sugar Planters' Sta., Div. Ent. Bul. 7, 1909.
[2] Hawaiian Planters' Record, 2 (1910), No. 2, p. 102.
[3] Hawaii Sta. Rpt. 1909.

Wireworm (*Simodactylus cinnamomeus*).
Tenebrionid beetle (*Epitragus diremptus*).
Cryptoblabes aliena.[1]
Batrachedra rileyi.[1]
Amorbia emigratella.[2]
Opatrum serratum.
Adoretus tenuimaculatus.
Araecerus fasciculatus.
Plodia interpunctella.
Ephestia elutella.
Setamorpha sp. (Reared by Swezey.)
Catorama mexicana. (Reared by Swezey.)
Nitidulid. (Reared by Swezey.)

WHEAT.

The following insects were observed attacking wheat:
Cutworm (*Agrotis crinigera*).[3]
Army worm (*Cirphis unipuncta*).[3]
Grass army worm (*Spodoptera mauritia*).[3]
Looper (*Plusia chalcites*).
Leaf roller (*Omiodes localis*).[4]
Corn leaf aphis (*Aphis maidis*).[5]
Opatrum serratum.
Epitragus diremptus.
Wireworm (*Simodactylus cinnamomeus*).

BARLEY.

The following insect was observed on barley:
Corn leaf aphis (*Aphis maidis*).[5]

JACK BEAN.

The following insects were observed on the jack bean:
Grass army worm (*Spodoptera mauritia*).[3]
Leaf miner (*Agromyza* sp.).

COTTON.[6]

The following insects were observed attacking cotton:
Cutworm (*Agrotis crinigera*).[3]
Grass army worm (*Spodoptera mauritia*).[3]
Cotton aphis (*Aphis gossypii*).[5]

[1] Hawaiian Sugar Planters' Sta., Div. Ent. Bul. 6, 1909.
[2] Hawaii Sta. Bul. 22, 1910.
[3] Hawaiian Sugar Planters' Sta., Div. Ent. Bul. 7, 1909.
[4] Hawaiian Sugar Planters' Sta., Div. Ent. Bul. 5, 1907.
[5] Hawaii Sta. Rpt. 1909.
[6] Hawaii Sta. Bul. 18, 1909.

Many of these pests are discussed in technical papers, in which life histories, remedies, natural enemies, etc., are given. References to these papers are made opposite the name of the insect. The following notes of observations at Kunia in connection with these crops are offered:

Cutworms and army worms undoubtedly did the most damage to the corn. Plants several weeks old in sections of the fields were so badly eaten that replanting became necessary. In other sections plants were literally stripped, both stalk and ear. The lower leaves were badly frayed and skeletonized by *Plusia chalcites* and the young larvæ of *Spodoptera mauritia*, but this injury is negligible. The corn leafhopper and corn leaf aphis are at times very injurious, especially to young plants. The ripening ears were attacked by *Cryptoblabes aliena*, *Amorbia emigratella*, and *Batrachedra rileyi*, which work in the silk at the flower end, also eating some of the cob. These insects attacking the standing corn are to be expected and can and ought to be systematically fought. For cutworms and army worms, the use of light traps in addition to poison bait is suggested. It might also be profitable to spray or dust the plants once or twice with arsenate of lead. The aphis and leafhopper may be sprayed with tobacco decoction, but they are difficult to control artificially.

The insects which attack matured ears or stored corn, such as the Angoumois grain moth, corn seed weevil, etc., can be best controlled by fumigating the stored corn. Corn stored in a tight bin may be fumigated with carbon bisulphid, 1 pound to 1,000 cubic feet; if the storeroom is not tight, the dose should be doubled.

Cutworms, army worms, and corn leaf aphis did the greatest damage to the wheat and barley, and in order to grow these grains it seems essential to control these pests in some way. The remedies suggested above are the only practical ones that can now be recommended, but the present situation might be greatly altered by the introduction of good parasites for this class of pests.

The dipterous leaf miner infesting jack beans gave this crop a very ragged appearance, and in sections the plants were eaten down to the ground by the army worm. The leaf miner is parasitized and is troublesome only at times. The army worm can be controlled with the remedies mentioned above.

The cotton aphis and climbing cutworms did the most damage to the cotton during the winter. The aphis was particularly bad, becoming so abundant as to cover both stems and foliage, and killing some plants. It is difficult to control by artificial means, but a spray of kerosene emulsion or tobacco decoction might be beneficial. Climbing cutworms should be fought with poisoned bait or by spraying with arsenate of lead.

In the spring the insects attacking the sweet potato were studied. The sweet potato is extensively cultivated here and is a staple article of food, especially among the Hawaiians and poorer classes. It has a number of insect enemies which damage the crop more or less, but do not prevent fair yields. The study was made as complete as possible within the limited time, life histories were obtained for most of the pests, and remedies elaborated. The results are now in manuscript and will later appear as a bulletin.

The most destructive pest of sweet potatoes apparently is the stem borer (*Omphisa anastomosalis*), a recent introduction from China. It bores into the stems and kills many plants. It sometimes gets into the potato, in which case the damage is even more serious. It is not much parasitized and is quite common in sweet-potato fields. It would be difficult to control artificially. The leaves of the sweet potato are mined by the larvæ of the tineid moth (*Bedellia orchilella*), and probably by other species of this genus, but this pest is fairly well kept in check by chalcid parasites. The hornworm (larva of the sphinx moth, *Phlegethontius convoluli*) is quite common but not often very injurious; cutworms are said to attack the sweet potato; and there are two leaf rollers (*Phlyctænia despecta* and *Amorbia emigratella*) which damage the foliage to some extent. The common sweet-potato weevil (*Cylas formicarius*) has at times been a very destructive pest and one difficult to control. It breeds in the stems of the common shore plant (*Ipomœa pes-capræ*), and will always be a menace to the cultivation of sweet potatoes, although actual instances of its infesting sweet-potato fields are few. Another weevil, the West Indian scarabee (*Cryptorynchus batatæ*), is also common in the tuber or rootstock of the sweet potato and at times greatly damages the crop. Among the minor pests may be mentioned the leaf hoppers *Nesosydne ipomœicola* and *Oloha ipomœa*, *Plusia chalcites*, an undetermined Pseudococcus, the Japanese beetle, and a species of Saissetia.

Considerable time has been spent in studying Coccidæ—a group of extreme economic importance in these islands—but no report can be offered on this work. An addition was made to the list of Hawaiian Coccidæ in recording the presence of *Geococcus radicum* Green on roots of mango, koa, and nut grass. The insect was described and figured anew by the writer.[1]

---

[1] Proc. Hawaiian Ent. Soc., 2 (1910), No. 3, p. 108.

A FIVE-YEAR-OLD AVOCADO TREE, TOP WORKED TO A SELECTED VARIETY BY BUDDING.

REPORT OF THE HORTICULTURIST.

By J. E. HIGGINS.

The work of this department for the fiscal year dealt chiefly with the avocado, mango, papaya, and citrus fruits. Minor attention has been given to the sweet potato and to a considerable number of miscellaneous subjects which demand recognition in the present stage of Hawaii's horticultural development.

AVOCADO.

The work with avocados during the year may be classified chiefly under four subjects, as follows: Propagation, insect control, disease control, and study of varieties.

PROPAGATION.

Substantial progress has been made in devising means for the successful budding of the avocado. Because of the lack of young nursery stock most of the trials have been in topworking of orchard trees. Plate I shows a tree in the experimental orchard topworked to a valuable variety by means of budding.

The greatest difficulty in budding appears to be not in getting the buds to unite with the stock, but in forcing them into growth. The sap of the avocado oozes out from incisions in the bark, and in budding this characteristic aggravates the difficulties. The sap finds an exit through the T incision, evaporates, and leaves here a crystaline deposit which frequently covers the whole bud, and sometimes the whole bud shield. This is particularly likely to occur before a union has been effected, although it may occur long after. It has been found possible largely to control this trouble, during the period when union is being effected, by wrapping the whole of the stock, in the region of the incision, and thus preventing evaporation.

When a bud has become united to the stock it has proved inadvisable to lop the stock immediately, as is done with citrus and some other budded stocks. The wood is often so brittle in the young portion, where the bud is inserted, as to prohibit successful lopping. If partly cut, it will snap off completely. If a stock is completely cut off, it is likely to die back to the bud and below it before the latter has started into growth.

To overcome these difficulties it has been found advisable to girdle the stock completely, or partly, at a point several inches above the bud, being careful to remove only the bark, so that the upper portion

25

will not be destroyed. Mr. Holt, who has done most of the actual manipulation of the buds under the direction of the horticulturist is continuing the work with a view of overcoming more completely some of the difficulties which have made the budding of avocados somewhat discouraging.

Inarching is being successfully used for certain types of propaga-. tion. It is quite easy to effect a union of scion and stock by this method, which presents a very ready means of bringing seedling varieties into early bearing by placing them on old trees. This may prove to be one of the best means of testing out seedlings whose characters it may be desired to determine, either for practical or scientific purposes.

Some success has been had in growing avocados from cuttings. It has frequently been found in the station experience that avocado cuttings readily form a callus, but do not strike root. The method which has proved partly successful in causing the formation of roots during the past winter consists in packing the cuttings in moist sphagnum moss for several weeks before placing them in the propagating bench. Thus far well-matured wood with gray bark has proved most promising in this work. If cuttings can be made to root readily there are occasions when this means of propagation could be advantageously used.

INSECT CONTROL.

The two chief insect pests of the avocado in the station orchards during the year have been the avocado mealy bug (*Pseudococcus nipœ*) and the larva of the tortricid moth (*Amorbia emigratella*). The latter has caused considerable damage to foliage in the station orchard and to the fruit in gardens of the city. The larva wraps itself up in the young leaves, sometimes sewing together the terminal leaves while opening. It inhabits this place until the food supply is somewhat reduced and then proceeds to another similar locality. Because its attack is upon the very newest growth it is not as easy to control by arsenical poisons as would otherwise be the case. However, frequent spraying with arsenate of lead has considerably reduced the numbers of these insects.

The avocado mealy bug for some years has not required much attention to keep it under control in the station orchard. Practically no spraying has been done for two or three years, and only an occasional tree has been fumigated. There are always some insects of this species in the orchard, but they do not appear to become a serious pest, probably being held in control by ladybirds. It is aimed to foster these by planting, every rainy season, a cover crop of cowpeas, jack beans, or some similar legume, which is subject to the attacks of aphides. These aphides do not disturb the avocado, but multiply in the legumes and furnish an abundant food supply for numerous species of ladybirds. After this food supply has been cut off, these natural enemies of the mealy bug turn their exclusive attention to the scale insects of the trees.

DISEASE CONTROL.

A fungus disease of the avocado, probably a species of Glœosporium, has done much damage in many parts of the Territory; in fact, no district has been visited by the horticulturist in which this disease has not been very prevalent. It attacks the leaves, causing them to become a rusty brown color, and frequently causing them to fall prematurely. It also causes the dying back of the twigs and branches and often results in the total destruction of the tree. During the past season, flowers were noticed destroyed apparently by this fungus, the destruction extending into the new wood. When the vitality of the wood has been reduced, it becomes an attractive place for borers.

Work has been begun to test the efficiency of four leading fungicides in the control of this disease. With these fungicides, arsenical poisons have been included, when possible, as a means of destroying the Amorbia mentioned above. The remedies being tried are: Bordeaux mixture with arsenate of lead (6–6–50 formula); resin lime mixture with Bordeaux (formula, 2 gallons resin lime stock to 48 gallons Bordeaux dilute); self-boiled lime-sulphur wash (6–6–50 formula) with arsenate of lead; and commercial lime-sulphur (formula 1–30), with arsenate of lead. It is too early to look for marked results from the use of these fungicides, since the work has been in progress only a short time. It can be said, however, that none of the remedies has produced any serious foliage injury.

VARIETIES.

Mr. Hunn, the assistant horticulturist, has made careful studies of a large number of varieties of avocados for the purpose of ascertaining their merits for commercial or home production. Many very excellent midseason varieties have been found. These, unfortunately, are not the best adapted to commercial growing, because they would reach the mainland when the markets were overstocked with many kinds of Temperate Zone and subtropical fruits. There is, however, a sale for such in limited quantities at high prices even at that season. First-class avocados in sound market condition will sell at that season of the year (June, July, and August) at $2 to $2.50 per dozen in the San Francisco market. The extra early varieties, which could be placed in mainland markets before the 1st of

June, and the extra late varieties which would be marketable after the 1st of November, could be sold in large quantities, as the demand for fresh fruit is better at that time. The four varieties following are of particular merit from one or another of the points of view indicated above:

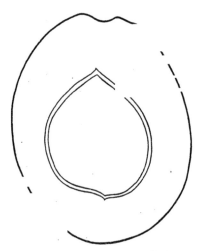

FIG. 1.—Form of fruit and seed of avocado No. 149. About one-fourth natural size.

No. 149 (Fig. 1). About 20 years ago Admiral Beardsley, leaving Guatemala for Hawaii, carried with him a number of avocados for consumption on the way. He saved two seeds, wrapping them in cotton wool and packing them in ice. Arriving in Honolulu, he gave one seed to Judge Wiedeman and the other to Mrs. E. K. Wilder. The former was planted at 1402 Punahou Street, now occupied by "The McDonald," and although both seeds grew, this one is far superior in quality and blooms earlier.

Form roundish to spherical; size medium to medium large; cavity small, shallow, and flaring; stem somewhat slender and very long, varying from 6 to 15 inches in length; surface undulating, very hard; coriaceous and markedly pitted; color dark olive green to purple, with small, very abundant, irregular-shaped yellowish dots; apex a mere dot, slightly depressed; skin very thick and woody, separating freely from the pulp; flesh yellow in color, running into green at the skin, fine grained, oily and somewhat buttery, 75 per cent of fruit; seed fairly large, roundish conical, just a trifle loose in the cavity; flavor rich and nutty. Season July to January.

The tree is quite vigorous, but tends to grow upward rather than to branch out, probably due to confinement. This pear is especially noteworthy, since it will keep for a long time after being removed from the tree. Mr. G. P. Wilder reports that he has kept the fruit for two and one-half weeks after removal from the tree. The tree carried fruit over through the blossoming period of the following season. Height 40 feet, spread 20 feet.

Valuable as a late avocado. Its woody skin should make it a good shipper.

MOANALUA (Fig. 2). A chance seedling 19 years of age growing on the estate of Hon. S. M. Damon, Moanalua.

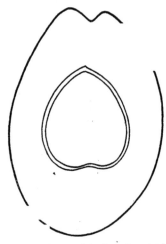

FIG. 2.—Form of fruit and seed of Moanalua avocado. About one-fourth natural size.

Form pyriform; size small to medium; cavity flaring, deep; stem somewhat short, rather thick; surface undulating, hard, coriaceous, and slightly pitted; color dark green, with medium abundant, small, irregular-shaped yellowish dots; apex a mere dot; skin medium thick, separating readily from the pulp; flesh yellowish in color, running into green at the rind, fine grained, melting and somewhat buttery, 70 per cent of the fruit; seed medium large, conical, fitting tightly in the seed cavity; flavor rich and nutty. Season July to September.

The tree is very vigorous. Height 30 feet, spread 25 feet.

No. 150 (Fig. 3). A chance seedling whose origin and age are unknown, growing near the residence of Charles Renear, Emma Street.

Form pyriform; size small to medium; cavity shallow and somewhat rounded; stem short and medium thick; surface undulating, medium hard, coriaceous, slightly pitted; color green, with reticulate-like markings, with medium large somewhat circular yellowish dots; apex a mere dot; skin very thin, separating readily from the pulp; flesh yellow, melting, but a trifle watery, 70 per cent of the fruit; seed medium large, conical, fitting loosely into the cavity; flavor pleasant. Season middle of May to July.

Valuable because of its earliness. Height 30 feet, spread 20 feet.

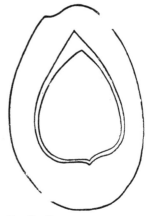

FIG. 3.—Form of fruit and seed of avocado No. 150. About one-fourth natural size.

No. 145 (Fig. 4). A chance seedling about 15 years of age; origin unknown.

Form pyriform; size small to medium; cavity shallow and somewhat abrupt; stem medium long and quite thick; surface undulating, hard, coriaceous, and slightly pitted and mottled; color green, with small, very abundant yellowish dots; apex a depressed dot; skin quite thin, separating fairly well from the pulp; flesh yellow, running into green at the rind, fine grained, oily, and somewhat buttery, 60 per cent of the fruit; seed very large, conical, fitting loosely in the cavity; flavor rich and nutty. Season September to January.

This tree is very vigorous and symmetrical. Height 25 feet, spread 25 feet.

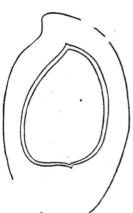

FIG. 4.—Form of fruit and seed of avocado No. 145. About one-fourth natural size.

FERTILIZER TRIALS.

The station orchard, consisting of miscellaneous varieties and many seedlings, makes it impossible to conduct an exact fertilizer experiment, but certain sections of the orchard have been chosen which apparently furnish sufficiently uniform conditions for some simple trials of fertilizers. It is hoped that these tests, conducted in cooperation with the chemical division of the station, will point the way to more definite and accurate experiments when uniform conditions can be attained. From our observations there is some evidence that the excessive use of nitrogenous fertilizers may tend to produce a fibrous fruit.

MISCELLANEOUS STUDIES.

Some studies have been made of the root system of the avocado. Attention has also been devoted to pruning, girdling, and other orchard operations.

MANGO.

PROPAGATION.

The propagation work with the mango has been continued along the lines outlined in previous reports and bulletins. Good use has been made of the method of shield budding the mango.[1] By this means a still larger number of new varieties have been worked in the trial orchard. Quite a number of potted trees have been taken to the orchard and have afforded inarches on some of the older seedling trees. A marked example of the results which may be obtained by this method has come into the station experience during the year. In December, 1908, an Indian variety, Brindabani, was thus grafted upon a strong seedling in the orchard. At the present writing, 18 months later, the new variety is bearing fruits nearly fully matured, others in various stages of development, and also flowers.

TRANSPLANTING.

Opportunity has been afforded for still further testing the possibilities of transplanting large nursery trees. Quite a number of 4 and 5 year old trees were taken up from the nursery and removed to the orchard, in part to test this matter, since it has frequently been stated that mango trees are difficult to transplant. All the trees were severely cut back, leaving only a trunk about $2\frac{1}{2}$ feet above the crown. The transplanting was done in the autumn and early winter, at a time when the trees were not flushing. Some of the trees were removed with naked roots and carefully taken at once to the orchard. Others were taken out with a ball of soil and planted immediately. Still another lot, which had been dug up 15 days previously and had been carefully " heeled in," were planted beside the others. A fourth lot, which had been treated in the same manner as lot 3 except that the naked roots were exposed to the air for an hour or two, was also planted. It has not been possible to detect any difference in the vigor of growth of any of the above lots, all trees having lived and made a good growth.

Mr. E. C. Smith, of Pearl City, Oahu, reports that he at one time removed a mango tree which had been bearing, and though severely cut back even the next year's crop was not lost. It appears, there-

---

[1] Hawaii Sta. Bul. 20.

fore, that if mango trees are transplanted when not in flush and are severely cut back a large degree of success can be expected in transplanting.

The above results of trials, together with the methods of budding the mango referred to, would seem to place beyond doubt the growing of the mango as nursery stock on a commercial scale

ROOT SYSTEM.

Studies have been made of the root system of the mango by sluicing away the soil and removing the tree with its main roots intact.

INSECT CONTROL.

It has been found necessary to fumigate a few trees in the mango orchard for the destruction of the scale (*Phenacaspis eugeniæ*) and also a few for the Florida red scale (*Chrysomphalus aonidum*). When the mango tree is not flushing it can be fumigated with hydrocyanic-acid gas in doses equal to those used on citrus trees without injury to the foliage.

A red-banded thrips (*Heliothrips rubrocinctus*) should be mentioned in this connection. These were found in large numbers on young mango seedlings in the greenhouse, and were causing very serious damage. They were referred to the station entomologist, who kindly had them identified as above. Those who are starting mango plants in greenhouses or in a sheltered place should be on the lookout for these pests. They may be distinguished as small, rather wedge-shaped bodies, very beautifully marked with red bands. It has not been found difficult to destroy them by dusting the plants with finely powdered sulphur after they have first been sprayed with water so as to retain the powder.

The species of Amorbia referred to elsewhere as a pest of the avocado has also proved destructive to the mango flowers and to some degree to the young leaves. Arsenate of lead has been found effective in destroying the larvæ.

The large carpenter bee (*Xylocopa œneipennis*) did considerable damage to young mango buds in the propagation experiments until its work was discovered and prevented. The bee seems to find an inviting place for boring just above the bud on the bud shield, and in many instances bored through the shield into the old wood of the stock, causing injury and sometimes destruction to the bud. It has been found easy to control this injury by placing grafting wax in all the incisions, leaving only the bud and a small portion of the shield exposed. This should be done when the bandage is removed, if injury of this kind is experienced.

DISEASE CONTROL.

The fungus (*Glœosporium mangiferœ*) does great injury to the mango crop in Hawaii, destroying the flowers and much of the fruit. It has been stated in earlier reports that this disease can be held in control by Bordeaux mixture. Experiments, however, have been undertaken with other fungicides for the control of this fungus. The same series of trials, as outlined elsewhere for the control of the diseases of the avocado, is in progress in the mango orchard.

VARIETIES.

There is now quite a large number of varieties in the station orchard. Some of these are introduced varieties from India and elsewhere, and others are valuable local seedlings. The list of varieties now growing at the station is as follows:

Alphonse, Accession Nos. 1072, 1158, 2014, 2101.

Douglas Bennett's Alphonse, Accession Nos. 278, 1161, 1370, 1371, 1926, 1933.

Ameeri, Accession No. 2100.

Arbuthnot, Accession No. 1943.

Bombay Yellow, Accession Nos. 1029, 1921.

Brindabani, Accession Nos. 1202, 1372.

Cambodiana, or Saigon, Accession No. 260.

Crescent, Accession Nos. 1945, 1946, 1948.

Divine, Accession No. 2108.

D'Or, Accession No. 2109.

Cowasjee Patel, Accession No. 2485.

Faizan, Accession No. 1200.

Fijri Long, Accession No. 1920.

French, Accession Nos. 1962, 1963.

Gay, Accession No. 1940.

Herbert's No. 9, Accession Nos. 1960, 1967, 1968.

Jamshedi, Accession Nos. 1201, 1373.

Java, Accession Nos. 1949, 1950, 1953.

Julie, Accession No. 2102.

Lady Finger Chutney, Accession No. 1271.

Mazagon, Accession No. 2484.

Mulgoba, Accession No. 2093.

Paheri, Accession No. 2094.

Peters No. 1, Accession No. 2092.

Pirie, Accession No. 1159.

Sharhati Black, Accession No. 1203.

Strawberry, Accession No. 1533 (local seedling).

Strawberry, Accession No. 1944 (from Section of Seed and Plant Introduction).

Sandersha, Accession No. 1074.
Totafari, Accession No. 279.
Smith Wootten, Accession No. 1985.
Wootten Chutney, Accession No. 840.

PAPAYAS.

MONŒCIOUS AND DIŒCIOUS TYPES.

Investigations have been begun with papayas which are of interest because of their bearing upon theories of plant breeding and also because of their practical aspect. It is a well-known fact that papayas are extremely uncertain in the reproduction of their characters. Selection has been practiced to a considerable degree by the growers of this fruit, but seeds from the best fruit are liable to produce trees of very indifferent character. The reasons for this may be suggested by a study of the different types of the papaya. There are two extreme types and several intermediate forms. First, there is the strictly diœcious type. In this, the fruit-bearing tree produces pistillate flowers only. The staminate, or "male," tree produces staminate flowers almost exclusively but with an occasional perfect flower which is capable of producing fruit. Most of the staminate flowers have a rudimentary ovary and style, but are without any stigma, and are utterly incapable of fruit production. The fruit of the pistillate tree of this type is usually ovoid or more or less rotund in shape.

The second type is monœcious. Every tree produces fruit. The trees produce two forms of flowers; first, a perfect flower, and, second, a staminate flower. In the axil of each leaf there is usually a small flower cluster, only a few inches in length, which contains at least one perfect flower and one or more staminate ones. This perfect flower is quite different in shape from the pistillate flower of the diœcious type. Its pistil is much more elongated, being almost cylindrical throughout a portion of its length. The stamens are usually situated on the inner walls of the petals, about midway of their length, with the anthers surrounding the lobes of the stigma. The fruit of this type differs from the fruit of the diœcious tree in the same way as the pistils. The fruit of this monœcious type is usually elongated, and is generally spoken of as the "long" papaya.

Between these two types, the one almost completely diœcious and the other monœcious, there are many intermediate forms which may have arisen through the crossing of these two. For example, there are in the station collection trees which produce three types of flowers, namely, staminate flowers and two forms of perfect flowers. The one form of perfect flower corresponds precisely with the per-

fect flowers of the monœcious type, spoken of above. The other perfect flower has an ovary in shape like that of the pistillate flower of
the diœcious type, and produces a fruit more nearly resembling this
type. Its stamens, however, are variously located; they may be
found at times arising from the base of the petals; or at times the
anthers are attached to the lobes of the ovary, the latter condition
usually resulting in a deeply furrowed or distorted fruit. One tree
in the station collection produces only staminate flowers, but is peculiar in the fact that these flowers are borne close to the stem and in
the axils of the leaves, while staminate trees of the ordinary diœcious
type produce their flowers in long pendant clusters.

BREEDING PROBLEMS.

What is the bearing of these facts to a practical plant breeder who
may wish to produce a papaya of a good variety whose characters
will be more or less stable in reproduction? Suppose that the
diœcious type is used in selection, as has been the case usually. Seed
from this fruit will necessarily be a cross of two individuals. The
characters of the female plant are known, but those of the male
plant are utterly unknown. The parent stock from which both came
may be known, but since there is wide variation in the fruit of two
pistillate trees from the same stock it is reasonable to suppose that
there will be the same wide variation in the male or staminate trees.
The variation between the pistillate trees can easily be determined
because their fruits are in evidence and can be tested; but the characters which are inherent in the male or staminate tree, and which
will be transmitted by it to its progeny, can be determined only
through the long process of actual hand-pollination, the sowing of
the seed thus produced, and the testing of the fruit. Even then,
what portion of its excellent or indifferent qualities it may have
inherited from its male parent can not be known. Furthermore, the
difficulty becomes aggravated by the fact that papaya trees usually
degenerate after a very few years. At least, pistillate trees usually
fail to produce good fruit after a few years of growth, although they
may continue to produce indifferent fruit for many years. Therefore, even if the inherent characters of the male or staminate tree
could be determined with reasonable accuracy, before any such determination could be made the tree would have become too old to be in
a reliable state of virility, if it degenerates as rapidly as the pistillate tree. It therefore appears reasonable to suppose that the process
of producing a stable variety of good qualities by the use of this
diœcious type would be extremely long and tedious. The hope, therefore, must lie in the use of the monœcious type. Here it is possible
to select an individual of known qualities. This may be used as the
sole parent stock, or may be combined with another parent of known

qualities. Of course, either may at the start be of uncertain reproducing power. That is to say, what mixtures of blood there may be in the individual at the start may not be known; but through repeated selections and the elimination of undesirable characters, it should be possible to produce a reasonably stable variety, provided, of course, that the stock is kept pure by constantly avoiding cross-pollinations, a process which is necessary in all plants reproduced by seed and whose flowers are subject to accidental cross-pollination.

A further practical difficulty in the use of the diœcious type, from the standpoint of the papaya grower, as well as the breeder, is the fact that a very large proportion of the trees from any given lot of seed are liable to be staminate, or males, and therefore useless, only a few trees being necessary to pollinate all the pistillate trees. It is impossible to distinguish the staminate from the pistillate trees in the early stages of their development. Various theories have been advanced to distinguish these two sexes before the trees have flowered, and it has been reported that staminate trees have been caused to produce pistils and fruits by beheading them. None of these means, however, has proved to be successful from a practical standpoint. Therefore, in any papaya orchard planted with the diœcious type, a very large percentage of the trees must be cut out after they have grown almost to maturity, resulting in unevenness and irregularity in the orchard and much loss of time and space. For this reason, together with the difficulties of breeding, the diœcious type will likely be largely eliminated.

Returning to the subject of papaya breeding, it is not yet known what the result will be from crossing the pistillate tree of the diœcious type with pollen from a tree of known character of the monœcious type. As has been indicated above, there are several intermediate forms which appear to be the result of crossing the monœcious and the diœcious types; but, apparently, there is no definite knowledge on this point. These intermediates may have resulted from the accidental crossing of the monœcious type with pollen from the staminate tree of the diœcious type. It may be possible to make some of these crosses without giving rise to an undue number of male or staminate trees.

This work which is only in its incipiency offers a wide and interesting field for investigation.

CITRUS FRUITS.

INSECT CONTROL.

No new problems have been undertaken with citrus fruits. The orchard is being maintained and has afforded opportunity for the further testing of fumigation with hydrocyanic-acid gas for the control of the mealy bug (*Pseudococcus filamentosus*) and other scale insects. This method of control has proved the most effective means which has yet been tried. It is extremely difficult to control *P. filamentosus* because it is so vigilantly attended by ants. It has been found possible to destroy the insects on the trees by fumigation if the soil is removed from the crown so as to expose the insects to the gas. Reinfestation, however, takes place more rapidly than in the case of the Florida red scale (*Chrysomphalus aonidum*) and the purple scale (*Lepidosaphes beckii*).

The caterpillar (*Amorbia emigratella*), referred to as a pest of mango and avocado, has required considerable attention. After consultation with the entomologist, treatment was begun with arsenate of lead. Because of the habit of this insect, in wrapping itself up in the newest growth, it becomes difficult to poison it with arsenical sprays. The spraying was repeated several times. The insect now appears to be fairly well under control.

NEW VARIETIES.

Several new varieties of oranges, pomelos, and lemons have been introduced during the year. A number of the newer Florida pomelos have been budded into the station orchards and nurseries. The station agronomist, Mr. F. G. Krauss, while traveling in Japan and China, collected some of the best pomelos of those countries, including the famous Amoy variety. Bud wood was brought back to Hawaii, and some of it arrived in fair condition. Buds were inserted in a number of stocks at the station, but none has succeeded. The buds "took," and a few started into growth but afterwards failed.

A number of citrus varieties have been received from Mr. Gerrit P. Wilder while traveling through the Orient and southern Europe. These have been worked into the nursery by both budding and grafting and are making good progress.

SWEET POTATOES.

In a bulletin of this station,[1] attention was called to the possibility of a profitable industry in the shipping of sweet potatoes from Hawaii to the mainland of the United States and Canada during the season when the market there is practically bare, because the home-grown product is out of season. All these markets are accustomed to the yellow variety, known on the Pacific coast as Merced Sweet. This local name has arisen from the fact that Merced is the center of the most successful sweet-potato cultivation. The variety is that usually known in the East as the Jersey Sweet. It was also stated in the

---

[1] Hawaii Sta. Bul. 14.

bulletin referred to that the red varieties commonly grown in Hawaii are unfamiliar to those markets. This left the question open as to whether Hawaiian sweet potatoes of the ordinary varieties would find a ready sale on the mainland.

This matter has been tested by the growing of a number of varieties and the marketing of the same in San Francisco. The first two shipments included several red sorts as well as the Merced. All varieties sold readily at 8 cents per pound. Later reports, however, brought out the fact that the dealers found the consumers prejudiced against the red color and refused to buy them. It would seem to be unwise for Hawaiian shippers to attempt to break down this prejudice, and attention should be given to the growing of the Merced variety, with which the market is familiar. Roots of this variety are being distributed by the station.

These trial shipments confirm the earlier belief that sweet potatoes of suitable varieties will bring high prices when the California product is out of season.

It seems hardly necessary to state that 8 cents per pound should not be expected on large shipments. The commission house which handled these trial lots advised the station as follows:

" If you can succeed in producing the yellow variety of medium to large size, we are confident they can be distributed here during our late spring and early summer season so as to make them quite profitable to you. By this we mean from 4 cents to 5 cents per pound with a possibility of higher prices for a portion of them."

The season of shipping is important. California sweet potatoes are out of season from about May 15 to August 1. This is the period during which Hawaiian-grown sweet potatoes should arrive. In some years it may be found possible to put them in a little earlier.

MISCELLANEOUS NOTES.

Quite a large amount of miscellaneous work presents itself from time to time, and miscellaneous plants of different species demand some attention. A few of these may be mentioned.

GARCINIA MANGOSTANA.

The mangosteen has one or two bearing trees to represent it in Hawaii. Two fruits, which represented half the crop of one of these trees, were secured a year or two ago. One of the two fruits contained a seed, which was planted and has made rather an indifferent growth, but has done better than plants which have been introduced in Wardian cases.

There are one or two other species of Garcinia in Hawaii which appear to do well. It has seemed probable that the mangosteen might do better in Hawaii if budded on other stocks. Mr. E. W.

Jordan secured bud wood of the mangosteen from Mr. Francis Gay, of Kauai, and the writer, in cooperation with Mr. Jordan, placed buds of these on the *Garcinia xanthochymus*, known locally as the "African mangosteen." This work was performed only a few weeks previous to the present writing, and it is therefore too early to know whether any successful results will arise.

CARISSA ARDUINA.

Carissa arduina (Ac. No. 1764, S. P. I. No. 11734), which is a South African fruiting shrub, was introduced from the Section of Seed and Plant Introduction of the Department of Agriculture in the year 1905 under the number indicated above. The four plants received at that time have all made a vigorous growth, but have exhibited decided differences in character. Two of the plants have proved heavy producers and two have been rather shy bearers. Plate II, figure 1, shows one of these trees in fruit.

The shrub is useful as a hedge plant because of its dense growth and its strong thorns, which render it practically impassable, and also for its very beautiful red fruits, which are about the size of a plum. The latter may be eaten from the hand or may be used in the manufacture of jellies.

Selections are being made of the best fruits from the two best trees. About 2,000 plants are now in the greenhouses and will be ready for distribution within a few months. There remains a large crop of fruit, affording the opportunity for still larger propagation and distribution. It is believed that the plant will be useful as a hedge to surround fruit gardens which are subject to the attacks of nocturnal visitors.

After the plants have become well established in the propagating houses they appear to be free from all serious insect attacks in Hawaii. They are subject to the attacks of the scale, *Saissetia hemispherica;* but this is so successfully parasitized in Hawaii by *Scutellista cyanea* and other parasites that it has not proved a pest on Carissa.

LITCHI (NEPHELIUM LITCHI).

A number of the plants of this species, introduced from China in 1908, have made a fair growth, although severely attacked by the Japanese beetle and by the scale (*Saissetia nigra*). The latter can readily be controlled by fumigation, and it is not believed that the Japanese beetle will prove a serious pest after the trees have grown to large size. The seedling litchis that are growing in various parts of Honolulu are not seriously attacked by this pest.

The litchi, being a slow grower and requiring usually from 15 to 20 years to come into bearing, when grown from seed in Hawaii, it

Fig. 1.—Carissa Arduina, a Valuable Fruit and Hedge Plant.

Fig. 2.—Pigeon Peas as a Windbreak for Nursery Stock.

has been thought desirable to attempt the growth of this tree on the more vigorous growing stock of the longan (*Nephelium longana*). Attempts are now being made to graft scions of these imported varieties on seedling longans by the inarching method.

DECIDUOUS FRUITS.

As stated in previous reports, the Parker ranch has undertaken rather extensive experiments in the growing of deciduous fruits and grapes. In these experiments the station has taken a considerable interest and has cooperated so far as possible. In February, 1910, the horticulturist again visited the chief of these plantings at Waiki, on the island of Hawaii, at an elevation of about 4,500 feet. Instruction was given in pruning, insect control, and the general care of the orchards, and observation was made of the progress of the different kinds of fruits being grown. This being the winter season, it was impossible to judge of the fruits themselves, except in the case of a few apples which had been kept through the winter. These were of good size, and those that were not withered by exposure to the air were crisp and of good flavor. Apples have made a very satisfactory growth, except those planted the previous season, which was one of unusual drought. Established trees seemed to do well, notwithstanding the prolonged dry weather. Peach trees also made a satisfactory showing and were reported to have produced good fruit. They were well supplied with fruit buds. Cherries have not succeeded, and plums and pears can not yet be said to have proved a success. Grapes of several varieties, including the Tokay and the Muscat, have made good growth and are reported to have produced fruit in 1909. In general, it may be said that the outlook is promising for the production of apples, peaches, and grapes in this locality.

TREE TANGLEFOOT.

This sticky substance has been used on the deciduous plantings, as well as on the station trees, for the purpose of preventing ants, cutworms, and other injurious insects from ascending the trees. Under some conditions it has proved quite effective if the surface is kept renewed by repeated agitations, or combings. A serious result appears to have followed the use of this remedy at the Waiki orchards on peach trees. It had been applied directly to the bark of the trunk and had remained for many months. Wherever it was found remaining upon the peach trees they were dead. Examination of the bark of the trunk under this sticky preparation revealed injury of the tissue and a discoloration which extended completely around the trunk. This remedy has been applied to the bark of a number of trees at the experiment station without any apparent injurious effects, but it has not been so applied to peach trees. It is, therefore, recommended that precaution be taken in its use, and that in the case of peach trees, particularly, it should not be applied directly to the bark. A broad bandage, made of cheap cotton dipped in hot paraffin, may be wound spirally around the trunk of the tree and tied at the top by splitting into two parts like a surgeon's bandage. To this the sticky substance may be applied without injury. If the cotton is not too strong there will be little danger of girdling.

PIGEON PEA.

The pigeon pea (*Cajanus indicus*) is being tested as a temporary wind-break and as a permanent wind-break for nursery stock. In two or three months from seed, it affords considerable protection to small growth, and in six or seven months attains a height of 6 feet, and thus makes a good wind-break for young citrus, avocado, and mango seedlings. For this purpose it is planted quite close in the row, the plants standing only 3 or 4 inches apart. In citrus nurseries, the rows of these fruit trees are being tried at 6 feet apart, and a row of pigeon pea is being planted midway between the citrus. Where land is cheap, it would be better to increase the distance between the rows. By this means the wind-break could remain as long as the trees might be in the nursery. Plate II, figure 2, shows the pigeon pea protecting young citrus seedlings.

RATTAN PALMS.

Several species of this palm, Dæmonorops, have been introduced from Java. About 200 of these palms have been distributed in different parts of Hawaii where it was thought they would be most likely to succeed. These plants afford a fiber which is used in the shipping of tobacco, and if successful in Hawaii should be a valuable aid to the tobacco industry.

BOUGAINVILLÆA DISEASE.

A disease of the bougainvillæa has been observed during the year on both the species *B. spectabilis* and the species *B. refulgens*. This is a sort of crown rot which causes the decay of the bark and wood near the ground. A large vine of *B. spectabilis* was treated by the removal of the dead bark and the washing of the wound with carbolic acid and water, after which paint was applied. The plant appears to be regaining vigor.

REPORT OF THE CHEMIST.

By W. P. KELLEY.

During the past year the chemical department has been engaged mainly in soil and fertilizer investigations along the lines suggested in the previous report. In addition, some attention has been given to a study of the composition of pineapples.

PINEAPPLE SOIL INVESTIGATIONS.

In the report for 1909 the writer pointed out some of the conditions that exist in the pineapple districts of Oahu and drew attention to their peculiarities. Investigations during the past year have further emphasized the necessity of a more intelligent management of these soils. Frequent requests by farmers for assistance and advice, together with numerous observations by the writer, have led to the conviction that the time has already arrived when special efforts must be put forth by the farmer if profitable yields of pineapples are to be maintained. The pineapple industry, important as it has become, is still in its infancy in Hawaii, and while continuing to hold out great promise, failure, or only partial success, has resulted in numerous instances. This fact, together with the scientific interest that naturally arises in connection with soils of such abnormal characteristics, justifies a thorough study of all the factors that influence the ultimate fertility of this land.

In numerous instances the application of various fertilizers in liberal quantities has not given satisfactory returns, and an increasing number of planters are realizing that something more than the addition of available plant food is demanded in their fields. The lack of drainage is evident, and in many instances a poor mechanical soil condition is apparent. With satisfactory yields on virgin soil the growers in many instances have failed to adequately appreciate the importance of maintaining what is called " condition " in the soil. In the main the land is under short-term lease, and the principal idea from the beginning of this industry has been to get out of the land a maximum crop at a minimum of cost, with little concern for the ultimate maintenance of the soil.

The work of this department in this connection has been directed along lines which are calculated to show the fallacies of the prevailing system and to secure a scientific basis for rational and permanent conservation of the soil. Looking to this end a series of field and laboratory investigations are under way which have already

41

resulted in data of scientific interest and of practical value, and when completed ought to enable the farmer to adjust his farm management so as to secure both profit from his efforts and a perpetuation of his business.

It is not considered necessary at this time to detail these investigations, as it is hoped to present this work in its entirety later in the year. The work is being directed toward a study of the effects of aeration, and the chemical and physical changes induced by continued cultivation are being studied in a systematic way. The nitrifying power of the soils, the decomposition of humus, and the physical and biological changes which develop at remarkable rates under the conditions that prevail are being given due consideration.

On Oahu, as previously pointed out,[1] the pineapple soils may be roughly classified as manganiferous and nonmanganiferous. The former, on account of their extreme abnormality, have received considerable attention. The extent of the black manganiferous soil is considerably greater than had been anticipated, and comprises an important part of the pineapple sections of this island. While the areas that contain 4 or more per cent of manganese are ill suited to pineapple growth, the results already obtained indicate that the areas which contain an intermediate percentage of this element may, by the use of suitable fertilizers, be cultivated in pineapples with fair success. The physical properties of the manganiferous soils are superior to those of the nonmanganiferous areas, and drainage is much better on these areas. Consequently if the toxic effects of manganese can be overcome, their cultivation in pineapples will be more permanent.

In one of the manganiferous fields a fertilizer test has been under way for sometime, and while some of the plants made fairly normal growth during their first year's development, with the return of winter and its incident low temperatures the pineapples became yellow and abnormal. Some of the plants, however, have partially regained a normal appearance during the warm weather of the past few months, and are now in full fruit. The plants treated with dried blood or ammonium sulphate, superphosphate or reverted phosphate, and sulphate of potash have from the first greatly exceeded all others, and while the yields will not be entirely satisfactory it suggests a possible treatment for soils that contain more limited quantities of manganese. This soil appears to be greatly benefited by the application of soluble phosphates,[2] although the chemical analysis shows that it contains a rather high percentage of this substance. Not all forms of phosphates, however, are effective. Basic slag produces an increased tendency to a yellowing of the plants, and usually results in poorer yields than no treatment.

[1] Hawaii Sta. Press Bul. 23.
[2] See Agr. Gaz. N. S. Wales, 21 (1910), No. 5, pp. 437, 438.

The popular idea concerning the black manganiferous soils has been that they are sour and therefore in need of lime, but chemical analysis has proven this view to be incorrect, and the application of lime to these soils almost universally results in the development of a more intense yellow color in the plant and its subsequent failure to produce fruit. Basic slag is known to contain free lime, and it is likely that its injurious effect may be traceable to this substance.

A thorough study of the solubility of manganese and the influence of fertilizing substances on its solubility, the form in which the manganese exists in the soil and its relation to pineapple failure, and the influence brought about by the growth of pineapples on the form of the manganese in the soil, the influence of manganese on nitrification, and the physiological functions produced by this substance in the pineapple plant have received considerable attention.

Other crops have been grown on this type of soil in pot cultures with varying degrees of success. Some of these showed abnormal appearances, especially during the first two months of growth. Cereals seem especially sensitive to an excess of manganese. Legumes, although showing normal root tubercles, grew poorly. The lower leaves turned brown and fell away. Cotton and root crops seem less sensitive to this substance than other plants. In practically all plants grown in this type of soil peculiar color appearances were developed, indicating that it reacts in some way on the chlorophyll. In some instances the chlorophyll is destroyed; in others, etiolin or xanthophyll are developed instead of the green coloring matter.

These experiments will be repeated during the coming year and other crops tried and a further study of the physiological functions performed by manganese will be made.

In connection with the pineapple soil investigations on Oahu, some attention has been devoted to a study of the soils in pineapple sections of Maui, where different soil and climatic-conditions prevail. Also, soil samples from Kula, the Parker ranch on Hawaii, and the Nahiku rubber district have been examined and some interesting results obtained.

RICE INVESTIGATIONS.

The fertilizer experiments with rice have been continued and some remarkably concordant results obtained. On account of the unreliability of a single year's test with fertilizers, the results of these experiments have not been published. It is customary with the Chinese rice growers in the islands to cultivate the same land in two crops of rice per annum, and where fertilizers are used generally only one application per annum, and that to the spring crop, is made. With the view of determining the residual effects on the fall crop from the spring application, the original plats in our experiments have been divided into two parts, one of which received an application to the spring crop only, the other the same application to both crops. These experiments have now been carried through three crops and preparations are now under way for the fourth. It is intended to make this a continuous fertilizer experiment, with the view of determining whether it is possible by the use of fertilizers to obtain satisfactory yields under continuous cultivation of rice. A rotation experiment, involving the use of fertilizers, is also being made. In addition, a series of plats, to which different forms of nitrogenous fertilizers were applied, was laid out and some very interesting results obtained. Some experiments [1] were made previously, which indicated that ammonium sulphate is the most economical form of nitrogen for rice culture. A duplication of these results has been obtained. The yields from the plats treated with nitrate of soda have consistently fallen far short of the yields obtained from the use of ammonium sulphate. This observation has led to a detailed investigation of the absorption of nitrogen by the rice plant.

In pot cultures, under strict chemical control, various forms of nitrogen have been applied and some remarkably interesting results obtained. Where the rice has access to nitrates, only very poor growth has resulted; whereas ammonium compounds have resulted in vigorous development. These experiments are being repeated and will likely form the basis for a publication later in the year.

The original practice of applying fertilizers when the rice is about two-thirds grown gave rise to a study of the absorption of nutrients by the rice plant at its several stages of growth. This investigation was carried through two crops with concordant results, and the complete data bearing on this subject have been published.[2] From the results obtained it would seem that the practice of late applications of fertilizers should be abandoned. A large percentage of the substances absorbed from the soil is taken up by the rice plant during its early growth, and greater economy is sure to follow the application of fertilizers before planting than can be obtained from making the applications at the time usually practiced. In connection with this investigation it has been shown that the composition of the rice plant may be materially affected by the application of soluble fertilizers: especially is this fact noticeable during the early development of the plant.

FERTILIZER EXPERIMENTS WITH COTTON AND RUBBER.

As announced in the previous report, two fertilizer experiments have been made with cotton. These are being continued with prom-

---

[1] Hawaii Sta. Rpt. 1907, p. 83.
[2] Hawaii Sta. Bul. 21.

ising results. The yields of the first crop were, in some instances, more than three times as great on some of the fertilized plats as on the checks, and the appearance of the cotton at present indicates a similar influence in the second crop. The upland soils of the islands for the most part are lacking in available phosphates, due largely to the insoluble nature of the soil phosphates. Some attention has been given to a study of the solubility of phosphates in different types of soils,[1] and the results thus far obtained indicate that the phosphoric acid of the soil is largely combined with iron and alumina as basic phosphates, and hence insoluble.

A fertilizer experiment with rubber was also begun, but sufficient time has not elapsed to draw conclusions regarding the effects. Fertilizer experiments previously made with this crop were limited in number and no extensive results have been published. The slow growth of latex-bearing plants suggests the importance of a practical means of hastening the time of commercial tapping. In this experiment not only the increased growth of the trees is being measured, but the rate of latex flow and the percentage of rubber obtained therefrom will be noted. The soil on which this experiment is located is rich in humus, but inadequately aerated, as is shown by the fact that practically all the iron compounds therein are in a ferrous state, which can not be considered desirable at least. An increase in aeration, due to cultivation, has already been shown to produce an enormous increase in the growth of the rubber trees, and it is hoped at a later time to make a systematic study of this point.

THE COMPOSITION OF PINEAPPLES.

The composition of pineapples grown in other localities has been pointed out by several investigators. In a study of pineapples from Florida, the West Indies, Bahama, and Singapore, Munson and Tolman[2] showed that neither the variety nor the locality in which the fruit is grown exercises any marked influence on its sugar content, although the ratio between reducing sugars and sucrose in a given variety was shown to vary considerably. One pineapple of the Smooth Cayenne variety, for instance, was found to contain 3.17 per cent reducing sugars (calculated as invert sugar) and 7.51 per cent sucrose, while another of the same variety contained 9.75 per cent reducing sugars (calculated as invert sugar) and only 2.98 per cent sucrose. Some analyses were recorded which showed abnormally low percentages of sugar. This fruit was shipped a considerable distance before being analyzed, and irregularities in composition, as pointed

[1] Jour. Indus. and Engin. Chem., 2 (1910), No. 6, p. 277.
[2] U. S. Dept. Agr., Bur. Chem. Bul. 87, pp. 31–38; Jour. Amer. Chem. Soc., 25 (1903), No. 3, pp. 272–280.

out by the authors, may, in part, be traceable to differences in the degree of ripeness at the time of gathering.

Recently Blair and Wilson [1] made an extensive study of the composition of pineapples as affected by the use of fertilizers, and pointed out some interesting results. No extensive investigation of the composition of Hawaiian pineapples, however, has been published, although this fruit is generally conceded to be superior in quality to that grown in most localities.

The Smooth Cayenne is almost the only variety grown in Hawaii, and on account of inadequate shipping facilities and the prevalence of certain fungi a large percentage of these pineapples are used for canning purposes. The fruit for canning is allowed to ripen thoroughly in the field; that used for fresh fruit shipment, on the contrary, is usually gathered just before the true ripening process begins. Some shippers maintain, however, that pineapples one-third ripe may be shipped as satisfactorily as the green fruit.

For the purpose of determining some of the facts regarding the composition of pineapples as influenced by the stage of ripeness at which they are gathered, a number of analyses have been made. The methods employed in this work are essentially those given under the Official Methods for the Analysis of Fruits and Fruit Products. [2] The reducing sugars were determined by the volumetric Fehling solution method; sucrose by double polarization, acidity by direct titration with tenth-normal potassium hydrate with the aid of phenolphthalein. The acid of pineapples is largely citric, but is expressed here as sulphuric. The total hydrolyzable carbohydrates were determined by digesting for two hours 50 grams of the crushed fruit with strong hydrochloric acid (sp. gr. 1.125), cooling, neutralizing with caustic potash, completing to 250 cubic centimeters, and filtering. Reducing sugars in the filtrate were determined by the use of the volumetric Fehling solution method and the results expressed as invert sugar. Nitrogen was determined by the ordinary Kjehdahl method and the solids in the juice were calculated by the use of the tables of H. Ellion from the specific gravity of the juice. Fiber was determined by the usual method for fiber determination in feeds.

The fruits used in this investigation for the most part were gathered from the field by the writer, and the stage of ripeness in every instance was noted, thus largely eliminating uncertainty as to this point. The analytical determinations for the most part were duplicated with concordant results. At this point thanks are extended to the growers in the several districts for their cooperation in this work.

---

[1] Florida Sta. Bul. 101.
[2] U. S. Dept. Agr., Bur. Chem, Bul. 107 (rev.), p. 77.

The following table shows the composition of pineapples that ripened normally in the field:

The composition of normally ripened pineapples.

Localities.	Serial No.	Nitrogen.	Acidity as H₂SO₄.	Reducing sugars calculated as invert sugar.	Sucrose.	Total sugars.	Polarization.		
							Direct.	Invert.	Temperature.
		Per ct.	*Per ct.*	*Per ct.*	*Per ct.*	*Per ct.*	*°V.*	*°V.*	*°C.*
Wahiawa		0.06	0.66	3.92	6.78	10.70	5	−3.6	31.7
Do	101	......	.56	3.94	7.97	11.91	6.4	−3.7	32
Do	105	.09	.43	5.10	7.54	12.64	5.8	−3.8	30.5
Do	110	.09	1.03	4.72	9.88	14.60	7.4	−5.1	32.3
Do	111	.07	.86	5.18	10.05	15.23	8	−4.7	32.7
Do	112	.07	.99	4.59	10.12	14.71	8.4	−4.4	32.3
Do	113	......	1.06	3.50	8.47	11.97	6.6	−4.2	30.3
Do	114	.09	.71	4.12	6.93	11.05	4.9	−3.9	31.4
Do	115	.07	.82	3.14	7.15	10.29	5.3	−3.8	31
Do	102	......	.53	3.84	8.36	12.20	6.9	−3.7	31.5
Ahuimanu	106	.08	1.05	3.86	9.45	13.31	7.7	−4.3	31.4
Do	107	.09	1.16	4.18	8.40	12.58	7.1	−3.6	30.8
Do	108	.08	.63	2.78	7.36	10.14	5.4	−4	30
Do	109	.09	.75	3.56	8.12	11.68	6.3	−4	31.7
Haiku	140	......	.45	4.35	6.08	10.43	4.2	−3.5	32
Do	141	......	.68	4	6.97	10.97	4.9	−4	30
Do	142	......	.63	4.87	6.47	11.34	3.9	−4.3	30.2
Do	143	......	.65	4.85	6.85	11.70	4.6	−4.2	28.6
Do	144	......	.61	5.55	6.03	11.58	4	−3.7	30
Average		.08	.75	4.22	7.84	12.06			

The above data show that Hawaiian pineapples vary considerably in composition. In general the acidity increases with the sugar content, and the average of the total sugars is about equal to that of pineapples from Florida and the West Indies.

In the following table is shown the composition of green pineapples, gathered just before the beginning of the ripening process:

The composition of pineapples just before the beginning of the ripening process.

Localities.	Serial No.	Acidity as H₂SO₄.	Fiber.	Solids in juice.	Hydrolyzable carbohydrates.	Reducing sugars calculated as invert sugar.	Sucrose.	Total sugars.	Polarization.		
									Direct.	Invert.	Temperature.
		Per ct.	*Per ct.*	*Per ct.*	*Per ct.*	*Per ct.*	*Per ct.*	*Per ct.*	*°V.*	*°V.*	*°C.*
Wahiawa	127	0.48	......	7.32	......	3.57	1.96	5.53	1.0	−1.5	30.5
Do	128	.44	0.19	5.92	5.00	3.17	.78	3.95	.0	−1.0	30.4
Do	131	.30	.16	......	5.07	3.36	.87	4.23	.4	−0.7	33.7
Do	132	.33	.17	......	5.10	5.03	1.88	4.91	1.3	−1.1	30
Experiment station	145	.39	......	7.44	8.02	3.33	3.14	6.47	2 5	−1.5	31
Average		.39	.17	6.89	5.80	3.29	1.72	5.01			

The above data are interesting as showing the low sugar content of pineapples at this stage of development. None of the fruit examined showed any yellow color, but in each instance the characteristic pale-green color around the basal eyes, which always makes its appearance just before the development of a yellow color, had developed. The appearance of this pale-green color, together with a flattening of the eyes, is the guide by which the fruit is selected for fresh-fruit shipment. The results show that green pineapples do not contain an excess of acidity or fiber, and from the percentages of hydrolyzable carbohydrates it is apparent that if the fruit is gathered at this stage it can never develop a normal sugar content. Numerous tests at all stages of ripeness have failed to reveal the presence of starch or dextrin in pineapples. It is noteworthy that the ratio of reducing sugars to sucrose at this stage is practically the reverse of that found in the normally ripened fruit.

With the view of determining what changes take place in the fruit in ripening after having been gathered green, a number of pineapples were held at the station until fully ripe. The time required for the completion of this process was usually about three weeks. The following table shows the results of this examination:

The composition of pineapples which ripened after being picked green.

Localities.	Serial No.	Acidity as H_2SO_4.	Fiber.	Solids in juice.	Hydrolyzable carbohydrates.	Reducing sugars calculated as invert sugar.	Sucrose.	Total sugars.	Polarization.		
									Direct.	Invert.	Temperature.
		Per ct.	*Per ct.*	*Per ct.*	*Per ct.*	*Per ct.*	*Per ct.*	*Per ct.*	*°V.*	*°V.*	*°C.*
Wahiawa	133	0.53	0.20	......	5.32	1.48	3.92	5.40	2.4	−2.6	30.7
Do	134	.60	.21	6.78	3.57	1.13	2.26	3.39	1.3	−1.6	28.4
Do	135	.55	.21	6.04	4.75	1.19	3.17	4.36	2.0	−2.0	32.8
Do	136	.63	.25	6.54	3.75	1.06	2.26	3.32	1.1	−1.8	29.1
Experiment station	146	.49	......	5.30	....	1.33	2.06	3.39	1.1	−1.5	32.4
Do	147	.39	......	5.13	....	1.27	2.03	3.30	1.0	−1.6	29.2
Do	148	.39	......	4.99	....	1.37	1.10	2.47	0	−1.4	31.4

The most important changes which took place in the ripening of these pineapples were the conversion of reducing sugars into sucrose, the development of flavor, and a breaking down and liquefaction of the tissues. True fiber and acidity were not materially changed.

The composition of pineapples, one-fourth ripe, is shown in the following table:

The composition of pineapples when about one-fourth ripe.

Localities.	Serial No.	Acidity as H_2SO_4.	Solids in juice.	Reducing sugars calculated as invert sugar.	Sucrose.	Total sugars.	Polarization.		
							Direct.	Invert.	Temperature.
		Per ct.	*Per ct.*	*Per ct.*	*Per ct.*	*Per ct.*	*°V.*	*°V.*	*°C.*
Wahiawa	126	0.62	7.34	3.03	3.79	6.82	2.8	−2.0	32
Do	129	.59	7.56	2.53	3.34	5.87	2.2	−2.1	28.4
Do	130	.59	8.36	2.83	3.83	6.76	2.6	−2.3	29.4
Experiment station	149	.72	9.20	2.77	5.89	8.66	4.5	3.0	30.8
Do	150	.75	10.93	2.56	5.25	7.81	4.0	−2.7	30
Average	....	.65	8.68	2.74	4.42	7.16	....	....	....

These data show that sucrose is developed at a considerable rate during the early ripening process, although the fruit at this time had stored up only about one-half of its normal sugar content.

The next table shows the composition of the fruit when it is approximately half ripe.

The composition of pineapples when half ripe.

Localities.	Serial No.	Acidity as H₂SO₄.	Solids in juice.	Reducing sugars calculated as invert sugar.	Sucrose.	Total sugars.	Polarization.		
							Direct.	Invert.	Temperature.
		Per ct.	*Per ct.*	*Per ct.*	*Per ct.*	*Per ct.*	° *V.*	° *V.*	° *C.*
Wahiawa	116	0.78	11.83	2.74	7.33	10.07	5.7	−3.6	31.8
Do	117	.67	10.36	2.61	6.70	9.31	5.0	−3.5	31.7
Do	124	.63		2.38	6.83	9.21	4.9	−3.8	30.5
Do	125	.54		4.16	6.09	10.25	5.0	−2.7	32.2
Average		.65		2.97	6.73	9.70			

There is a rapid accumulation of sucrose in the ripening of the pineapple. If the fruit is picked at the half-ripe stage and allowed to ripen thoroughly, it will develop a normal flavor and be a highly desirable product.

From the foregoing data it is shown that green pineapples contain a small percentage of sugars, and if gathered at this stage never develop into desirable fruit. As the ripening process proceeds normally, sugars are stored up at a rapid rate, so that by the time the fruit is half ripe it contains a fairly high percentage of both reducing sugars and sucrose; and if gathered and allowed to ripen will mature into a highly edible fruit. The acidity of green pineapples is practically the same as that of the ripe fruit, whereas the ratio of reducing sugars to sucrose is reversed.

As pointed out above, the changes in pineapples that ripen after having been gathered are those of rearrangement, rather than the production of sugars. The composition of the fruit shows that it contains no substance of any consequence that could be converted into sugars, and therefore the total sugar content of pineapples does not increase after being gathered. It is a recognized fact in plant physiology that sugars may result from two different processes—first, from the direct action of chlorophyll in the chlorophyll-bearing cells, and secondly, from a breaking down of other carbohydrates. In some instances there is an accumulation of starch in plant organs which later is hydrolyzed into sugars. In the pineapple, since starch was never found in the fruit, it is safe to conclude that the sugar stored up in normally ripening pineapples is manufactured in the chlorophyll-bearing cells of the leaves and then transferred to the fruit;

hence when the fruit is severed from the stalk all communication with the source of sugar is broken, and therefore its accumulation is permanently stopped.

The cells of green pineapples, as seen under a high-power microscope, contain a thickened layer on the interior of the cell walls, and it is with difficulty that the juice is expressed from the cells. As the ripening process proceeds this thickened layer is gradually dissolved until at maturity the cell walls are extremely thin and easily ruptured. If pineapples are gathered green and allowed to ripen, it has been found that there is a dissolving of this thickened coat on the cell walls, thus apparently increasing the percentage of juice in the fruit without materially changing the concentration of the juice. Later a microchemical study of these changes will be made.

Thanks are extended to Dr. Wilcox for advice and many suggestions in this work; also to Miss Alice R. Thompson for valuable analytical assistance.

By F. G. KRAUSS.

Problems affecting the culture of rice and cotton continue to be the main lines of inquiry of this division, as for several years past.

RICE INVESTIGATIONS.

IMPORTS AND EXPORTS.

The increasing importations of rice from Japan, which amounted to 27,886,102 pounds, valued at $717,064 in 1909, as against 9,656,796 pounds, valued at $221,116 in 1905, has resulted in a gradual and finally a marked decrease in the production of this important crop in Hawaii.

The following table gives the United States customs statistics covering the imports and exports of rice to and from Hawaii during the period referred to above:

Imports of rice into Hawaii.

Year.	Japan.		China.		United States.	
	Amount.	Value.	Amount.	Value.	Amount.	Value.
	Pounds.	*Dollars.*	*Pounds.*	*Dollars.*	*Pounds.*	*Dollars.*
1905	9,656,796	221,116	11,964	245	9,983,491	303,029
1906	12,496,396	283,653	22,600	529	4,129,643	164,683
1907	21,012,842	539,021	13,906	351	755,050	34,144
1908	26,695,642	740,975	6,485	155	95,524	4,821
1909	27,866,102	717,064	13,966	314	109,300	4,358

The exports to the United States from Hawaii during the same period were:

Exports of rice to the United States from Hawaii.

Year.	Amount.	Value.	Year.	Amount.	Value.
	Pounds.	*Dollars.*		*Pounds.*	*Dollars.*
1905	2,771,083	84,414	1908	3,038,624	140,768
1906	5,739,500	223,012	1909	5,823,585	255,210
1907	3,324,107	147,439			

These inroads upon one of Hawaii's staple products are not based upon a competition in prices, but upon quality. The imported product sells at from 25 cents to $1 more per 100 pounds than does the locally grown rice. The Japanese, who are the principal consumers of rice in Hawaii and the sole importers of the Japan products, de-

51

mand a distinct type of rice whose characteristic culinary qualities are inherent in certain varieties, and also in large part due to the conditions of growth.

RICE IN JAPAN.

With a view of determining, if possible, the varieties and cultural conditions under which the preferred Japan rices are grown, the writer was authorized by the United States Department of Agriculture to undertake such investigations. Accordingly, the fall months of 1909 were devoted to a critical study of the industry in Japan. Valuable data were obtained at several experiment stations, of which the Central Experiment Station at Nishigahara (near Tokyo), the Kinai Branch Station at Kashiwara (near Osaka), and the Kiushiu Branch Station at Kumamoto (in the famous rice region of Kyushu) are worthy of special mention. The last two stations are devoted almost wholly to rice investigations.

At the Kinai Station a fine opportunity was offered to study varieties. Here have been brought all the types of rice grown in the Empire. After six years' study and comparison these have been grouped under 600 more or less constant varieties or strains sufficiently distinct for classification. A hundred of the most distinct types were obtained for experimental purposes, and are now under comparative tests with the best Hawaiian varieties. After inquiry among rice specialists and personal study, the four following standard varieties were determined upon as most promising for Hawaiian conditions, from both culinary and cultural standpoints. The varieties Omachi and Shinriki are the two types now almost exclusively exported to Hawaii, as they find special favor among the large Japanese population, and bring the highest market prices. The varieties Benkei and Miyako are considered of the highest quality in Japan, and are in great demand by those who can afford to buy them. A hundred pounds of choice seed of each of the four varieties were obtained for distribution among Hawaiian growers. Eight prominent growers availed themselves of seed for this spring's planting, and reports of the results of their experiments are now looked for.

The following descriptions of the above varieties are based on a study of pure strains made in the field at the Yamaguchi Demonstration Station, which is situated in the center of the region from which nearly all the Japan rice entering Hawaii is imported, and where these particular varieties are said to attain their highest perfection. A comparison of the behavior of these varieties grown at the station rice trial grounds during the past spring, from the identical stocks described above, should be of value as determining their adaptability to Hawaiian conditions, from the cultural side, at least. Their culinary qualities are, of course, as yet to be determined, and upon this will depend their acceptability to the consumer.

DESCRIPTION OF FOUR NEWLY INTRODUCED JAPAN RICES (PLATE III).

1. Miyako. Average height of plants, 48 inches; inclined to lodge; average number of fruiting culms per clump, 16; panicles large and compact; kernels medium size, awnless; a fair yielder, medium early. Considered the very best variety grown in Japan.

2. Benkei. Average height of plants, 40 inches; stands up well; average number of fruiting culms per clump, 18; panicles compact and heavy; kernels large, awnless; good yielder, early maturing. Considered a promising new variety in Japan, of fine culinary qualities.

3. Omachi. Average height of plants, 48 inches; slightly inclined to lodge; average number of fruiting culms per clump, 15; panicles large but rather loose; kernels medium size, awned; yields well; a type not likely to be appreciated by the Hawaiian grower because of its awned glumes; but strongly recommended by the Japan experiment stations for trial. It is a standard variety of Japan; extensively exported to Hawaii.

4. Shinriki. A standard variety in Japan; largely exported to Hawaii. Of more recent development than Omachi and by some considered an improvement. Average height of plant, 42 inches; stands up well; a heavy tillering sort, averaging 20 to 30 fruiting culms per clump; panicles small to medium; kernels small, awnless; good yielder; classed as a late variety in Japan, but the writer found it maturing at about the same time as the other varieties described above. Considered by the writer a promising variety for Hawaii.

The table below gives the results of the first season's cultural trial of the above varieties in comparison with the old type of Japan rice heretofore grown to a limited extent in Hawaii. The seed was sown February 4, the seedlings transplanted March 15, and the crop harvested June 3, 1910, the growing period being 119 days for all varieties.

Comparative tests of new and old types of Japan rice (spring crop, 1910) grown without fertilization.

Name of variety.	Average height of plants.	Average number of fruiting culms.	Yield of paddy from 100 clumps.	Yield of straw from 100 clumps.	Character of glumes.
New types:	*Inches.*		*Pounds.*	*Pounds.*	
Benkei..........................	28	16.2	4.0	3.28	Awnless.
Miyako..........................	33	16.7	3.75	3.53	Do.
Omachi..........................	31	17.8	4.87	3.61	Awned.
Shinriki..........................	26	23.1	4.23	3.06	Awnless.
Old type:					
Japan rice No. 153..........................	29	19.8	4.15	4.62	Do.

In comparison with the old type Japan rice, No. 153, both Omachi and Shinriki, the two standard sorts in Japan, which are the only varieties imported into Hawaii, outyielded the former. This is in itself a distinct gain should the quality be maintained in future culture. The variety Benkei, which especially appealed to the writer from a cultural standpoint as he saw it growing in Japan, did not quite equal the yield of the old type, but seems promising. Miyako, considered the best type of rice grown in Japan, gave the smallest yield. It is also considered a rather light yielder in Japan, but its superior quality and consequent high price makes it a leading sort in favored localities. The heavy tillering qualities of Shinriki appear to have been maintained in this trial. From the standpoint of yield, it would appear that Omachi and Shinriki are the most promising sorts. The main objection of the Hawaiian grower to the former variety is its bearded glumes. The Japanese have effected a cross between these two varieties with a view to inducing heavier tillering, beardlessness, and the superior flavor of Omachi in the hybrid. The two former qualities have been effected to a marked degree. Sufficient stock of the hybrid has not yet been grown to make a culinary test. The station was fortunate in securing a small quantity of this hybrid seed for trial.

The figures in Plate III show typical panicles of the several rices just described, and in addition, the variety Saratama, a promising variety, which, owing to its late maturity, can not be described in this report. Panicles of less acceptable types of Japanese rices are shown in Plate IV.

SELECTION AND BREEDING.

In addition to the variety tests of new Japanese and Chinese rices, noted above, the development of pure strains of the best old type is being continued. Some of these strains are now in the seventh generation of selection. A number of these show a marked improvement over the original type, as shown in comparative cultural tests. Increase in yield has been less noticeable than greater purity and uniformity.

Unfortunately, much difficulty has been experienced in inducing growers to perpetuate improved station strains in a pure state. Only limited quantities of station seed are available for distribution, so that growers are dependent upon themselves to produce such seed as they may need for general plantings. However, a season or two of commercial culture almost invariably results in a mixture of varieties. Aside from immediate local benefits, the importance of maintaining pure strains of high-bred rices is well illustrated by a request which came from a rice broker in New Orleans. The station was applied to for samples of choice seed in the hope that a select Hawaiian stock could be obtained to replace the large importations of South American seed used for planting. This is owing to the prevalence of red rice in American seed. A number of local growers submitted samples, but the only stock acceptable was a station strain, for which a substantial advance over current local prices was offered, if obtainable in carload lots. However, too limited an amount was available to make it an object to the purchaser. This experience appears to have renewed the interest in the possibility of growing rice for seed purposes, which has been urged persistently by the

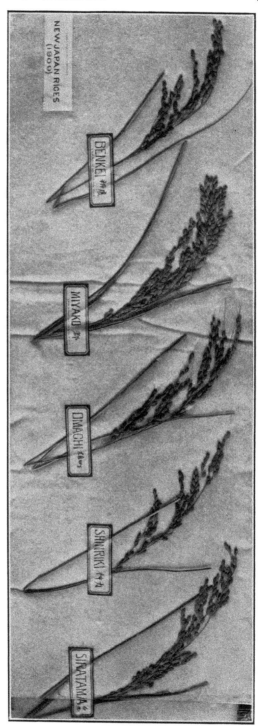

TYPES OF RICE CONSIDERED OF HIGHEST CULINARY QUALITY IN JAPAN.

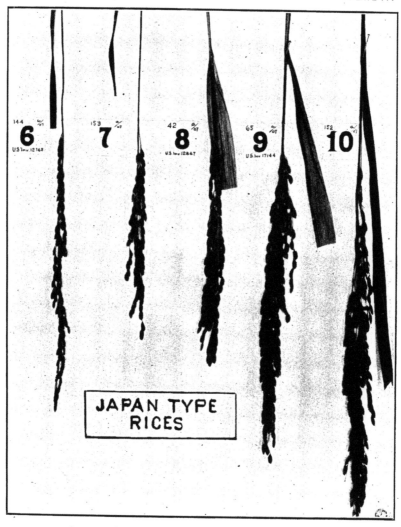

JAPANESE RICES NOT ACCEPTABLE TO JAPANESE CONSUMER.

station. One grower has asked the station's cooperation in developing this phase of the industry.

Of the several new varieties of rice introduced by the station in past years, variety No. 19 (S. P. I. No. 12508), introduced in 1907, appears to have at last found favor among the more intelligent growers. The Oahu rice mill of Honolulu reports having milled 480 bags, equivalent to 24 tons, during the past season. Other growers and millers are yet to be heard from. Mr. A. Hanneberg, of the Kaneohe Rice Mill Co., who produced several hundred bags of the above lot, speaks enthusiastically concerning this variety and states that it is well suited to the salt-marsh lands, which heretofore were devoted only to inferior rice. Should its adaptability to salt lands and a maintenance of high quality hold true in subsequent practice, a valuable acquisition will have been added to the resources of Hawaii.

Because of the exceptionally heavy tillering, together with the desirable hard, translucent grain of rice No. 19, efforts have for several years past been made to effect a cross between it and the best type of Hawaiian Gold Seed. The latter variety still remains the standard sort with the white and Chinese population, in addition to being one of the leading varieties of export. Could heavier yields and a clearer grain be obtained in Gold Seed, on the one hand, and the fixed property of fall maturity of rice No. 19 be changed to the "all season" cropping habit, which characterizes the Gold Seed, valuable combinations would be effected.

The difficulty thus far has been to get the two varieties to flower at the same time to permit of cross pollination. As the habits are now so well known, it is believed that the extensive plantings planned for this fall will provide the necessary conditions for hybridization.

A careful study was made of the methods practiced by the Japanese in their rice breeding, which has proved very successful during recent years. It is believed that valuable data were obtained as an aid to the contemplated work at this station.

In the study of tens of thousands of individual plants annually by Japanese investigators a natural hybrid among rice was found to be of rare occurrence, notwithstanding the fact that more than 600 varieties have been grown in close proximity for several years past. These results are in agreement with the writer's findings, but contrary to the generally accepted theory.

ROTATION.

The fertilizer investigations with rice having been assigned to the chemical division, this division has had to do with cultural work only. This has included, during the past spring experiments in crop rotation and green manuring, the latter in cooperation with the chemical division. Barley, one of the cereals extensively used in rotation with rice in Japan, and the established Hawaiian legumes, cowpeas, soy beans, velvet beans, and jack beans (*Canavalia ensiformis*), were planted as rotation crops during the spring, together with the Japanese and Chinese matting plants (*Juncus effusus* and *Cyperus tegetiformis*), which the station has been growing for several years. In addition to the above legumes used as rotation crops, there were planted as green manuring crops *Astragalus sinicus* (the "Genge" or "Renge" of Japan) and *Vicia faba*, the two green-manuring plants most extensively used for rice in Japan. The barleys, of which 50 of the best hulled and naked Japan paddy field varieties were sown, did poorly as a whole, a large percentage failing to head. Some 20 varieties set seed and appear to be fair yielders of grain. All are of very dwarf type, averaging less than 24 inches to tip of spike. Being planted in March, the lateness of season may have had considerable to do with this first poor showing.

Large quantities of barley are imported into Hawaii and its profitable culture in the islands would add materially to their resources. Furthermore, a rotation of a dry-land crop with the submerged culture of rice could not but prove beneficial to the paddy soils, as has been found to be the case in other countries.

The Astragalus used for green manuring proved an entire failure. Planted in March, the seed germinated well, but failed to make more than the feeblest growth. This persisted till the flowering stage and then wasted away, notwithstanding an ample supply of moisture.

The Windsor beans made quite a vigorous growth, but, as in former experimental plantings, failed almost wholly to set seed. It is already quite evident that these two types of green-manuring plants should be planted late in the fall during the coolest season of the year and under moist conditions, such as prevail in paddy fields.

The older-introduced legumes all did well and yielded a large amount of organic matter. Planted in March, the following results were obtained, calculated to acre yields.

Plat III: Soy beans. Variety, Mammoth Yellow; days to turning-under stage, 63; height, 24 inches; yield of green vegetable matter (including main roots), 10,125 pounds; yield as cured fodder (including seeds), 2,500 pounds; yield of seed, 675 pounds; distance of rows, 24 inches.

Plat IV: Velvet beans (*Mucuna utilis*); days to turning-under stage, 75; height of main growth, 28 inches; yield of green vegetable matter (including main roots), 15,300 pounds; yield as cured fodder, 3,420 pounds; yield of seed, 145 pounds; distance of rows, 4 feet.

Plat VII: Cowpeas. Clay type; days to turning-under stage, 75; height of main growth, 36 inches; weight of green vegetable matter (including main roots), 32,400 pounds; yield as cured fodder, 7,200 pounds; yield of seed, 1,417 pounds; distance of rows 4 feet.

Plat VIII: Jack beans (*Canavalia ensiformis*); days to turning-under stage, 75; height of plants, 40 inches; yield of green vegetable matter (including roots), 17,000 pounds; yield as cured fodder, 4,060 pounds; seed not mature at this writing; distance of rows, 4 feet.

Planted March 1, a part of each of the different varieties was turned under about the middle of May, excepting the soy beans, which were turned under 10 days earlier. The jack beans were much the latest to mature, but were turned under with the others to permit of uniform decay before planting the succeeding rice crop.

As will be noted from the above, the cowpeas considerably out-yielded all the other legumes, both in green matter and seed. This is in concordance with a number of previous tests in which many different kinds of legumes were under trial. However, both the velvet bean and jack bean are much surer croppers, being practically immune from the attacks of aphis to which the cowpea is especially subject. The main objections to jack beans and velvet beans are their slow maturity and less palatability. The soy bean, because of its early maturity, lends itself well to short seasons and will often fit in where legumes of larger yield but slower maturity would be out of the question.

The matting plants have not yet been harvested, but their growth compares favorably with that previously reported.

COTTON EXPERIMENTS.

Although still in the experimental stage, the cotton industry in Hawaii has made substantial progress during the past year. Many inquiries have come to the station concerning varieties and methods of culture. Station seed has been widely distributed for experimental purposes, enough being sent out to plant several hundred acres. It is estimated that fully 500 acres are now planted in the Territory. The largest planting comprises about 80 acres. The first commercial crop has been harvested, and is now in bale awaiting shipment. Samples submitted to experts have been pronounced first class; the highest market prices have been quoted.

As announced in the Annual Report for 1909, two extensive co-operative experiments on a field scale were begun in the early part of 1909. The first harvest of these has been completed, and the results, although far from satisfactory from the commercial side, are nevertheless of great value from an experimental point of view.

KUNIA COOPERATIVE COTTON EXPERIMENT.

Kunia lies on the east approach to the Waianae Range, at an elevation of about 600 feet. The soil is a deep, light, silty loam. The region would be classed as semiarid, the rainfall averaging less than 20 inches. The natural growth is guava, lantana, klu, and an occasional large kukui tree, Opuntia and algaroba. The grasses are rather sparse, but manienie, piipii, and other native grasses are met with. The whole growth is characteristic of dry regions. No previous crop had been grown on the lands under experiment.

Preliminary to the experiment the land was plowed in October of the previous year to a depth of at least 24 inches, several times harrowed, and finally plank-dragged, which left the soil in fair condition for planting.

On February 16–19 one-fourth acre was sown to each of the following varieties, Caravonica " wool " (Plate V), Egyptian (Mit Afifi), Sea Island (Georgia and Florida strain), Sea Island (" Seabrook "), and upland " Chinese," as an early planting; and a month later another one-fourth acre was sown as a late planting. All varieties were planted 2½ by 5 feet apart, giving 3,480 plants per acre, except Caravonica, which was planted 5 by 10 feet apart, or at the rate of 870 plants per acre. Each plat consisted of an additional half acre, a third of which was left fallow, a third planted to jack beans as a green manuring or rotation crop, and the remaining third was planted to soy beans and cowpeas. This half of each acre plat was then to be followed with cotton in the succeeding year; thus, in the second year (1910), a comparison between 1 and 2 year old cultures was obtained.

The results of the first year's harvests are given in the following table:

Yields of cotton from first year's harvest, Kunia cooperative experiment.

Plat No.	Variety.	Yield of seed cotton.		Yield of lint.	Yield of seed.	Percentage of lint to seed.	Quoted market value of lint.
		Weight at picking (¼ acre).	Weight after 6 months (¼ acre).[1]				
		Pounds.	*Pounds.*	*Pounds.*	*Pounds.*	*Per cent.*	*Cts. per lb.*
I.	Caravonica "wool":						
	Early planting................	32½ }	54	. 24	30	44. 4	0. 29
	Late planting.................	22 }					
II.	Egyptian, Mit Afifi:						
	Early planting................	95 }	131	44½	87	33. 3	. 29
	Late planting.................	37½ }					
III.	Sea Island, Georgia-Florida strain:						
	Early planting................	107 }	169	50½	170	29. 4	. 31
	Late planting.................	64¼ }					
[2]IV.	Sea Island, "Seabrook":						
	Early planting................	397¾	392	106	236½	30. 8	. 31
V.	Upland, "Chinese":						
	Early planting................	115½ }	211	71	140	33. 6	. 15
	Late planting.................	119¼ }					

[1] After the first weights were taken the cotton harvested from the early and late planting of each variety was unintentionally bulked together; hence, the cured weights represent the yield of the two plantings—the product of a half acre. To calculate to acre yields, multiply separate plantings by 4, and the totals of the 2 plantings by 2.

[2] Plat IV, consisting of 1 full acre of early planting, was divided into 13 sections for a fertilizer experiment, the detailed results of which will be reported by the chemist in a later bulletin.

The low yields from this experiment may be attributed to several causes. The rainfall, amounting to about 22 inches for the year, was doubtless inadequate for optimum growth on rough and newly

FIG. 1.—CARAVONICA "WOOL" COTTON 6 MONTHS FROM SEEDING.

FIG. 2.—CARAVONICA "WOOL" COTTON 9 MONTHS FROM SEEDING.

COOPERATIVE COTTON EXPERIMENTS.

FIG. 1.—PRUNING 1-YEAR-OLD CARAVONICA "WOOL" COTTON.

FIG. 2.—SECOND SEASON'S GROWTH OF CARAVONICA "WOOL" COTTON.

COOPERATIVE COTTON EXPERIMENTS.

broken ground. Although the germination was excellent, cutworms attacked the young seedlings from their very appearance above ground, destroying as high as 80 per cent of the stand in some cases. This necessitated repeated partial reseeding. In the case of the early plantings, four reseedings were made, and in the late plantings, two reseedings. These reseedings ranged from 20 per cent upward. It will be noted that the late plantings gave much lower yields than the early plantings, and this gives further proof that the great decrease in yield is due to irregularity of stand. It is safe to say that the original early planting outyielded any subsequent plantings twofold, so that a full stand of the first seeding would unquestionably have given fair yields as judged by mainland standards.

Comparatively little damage was traceable to the bollworm. But during the latter part of the season this pest was much in evidence among the general plantings of the development company, whose cotton fields surrounded the experimental plats. The fertilizer experiments gave good evidence of the value of proper fertilization, as has already been pointed out by the chemist in his report.

The importance of selecting suitable varieties is not fully brought out by the table of yields, but a study of the plants in the field indicates that the Upland type, while slightly outyielding the next best in point of yield, gave insufficient increase to make up for the difference in price.

The Egyptian cotton showed fine individual plants, but the poor stand reduced the acre average below all other varieties, except the Caravonica. This latter variety, as is well known, yields poorly the first year, even under favorable conditions.

The best sections in the fertilized Sea Island plat, as well as the best plants in Plat III, containing another strain of Sea Island, give promise for this variety in seasons of average rainfall. This variety should receive further consideration, because of the high quality maintained by the fiber under adverse conditions of growth.

Judged from the standpoint of general growth, and the subsequent heavy squaring of the Caravonica cotton, this variety unquestionably gives the greatest promise as a drought resister, and would seem the variety especially adapted to this locality. Plates V and VI give a series of views of the Caravonica plat. Figure 1, Plate V, illustrates the growth attained at six months from seed. Figure 2 shows the beginning of the harvest, nine months after planting. While the plants as a whole yielded an average of less than 3 ounces per plant, owing to poor stand and irregularity of the remaining plants, a number of selected specimens yielded over 1 pound per plant. Figure 1, Plate VI, shows the partially dormant plants twelve months after planting, as they were being pruned. Figure 2 of the same plate shows the same plants at the present writing, about eighteen months from time of planting. The plants are heavily loaded with squares, blossoms, and young bolls, from 100 to 500 fruits in the different stages having been counted per plant. Although less than 6 inches of rain has fallen in the past half year, the plants are growing vigorously, and with every prospect of giving a good yield. It is interesting to note that the irregularity in the size of the plants, presented in the first year, has largely been overcome during the fore part of the second season. All vacant places have been filled in by transplanting one-year old stocks which, with few exceptions, are growing well.

On the basis of the results of the past season the company controlling these lands have added 50 acres of Caravonica to the previous plantings, making a total of about 75 acres.

WAIPAHU COOPERATIVE COTTON EXPERIMENTS.

The Waipahu cooperative cotton experiment is located on the uplands bordering the edge of the upper irrigated cane lands of the Oahu sugar plantation, which faces the Koolau Range. This experiment is a duplication of the Kunia experiment, excepting that the entire acre of each experimental plat was sown in two plantings, instead of half that amount, as at Kunia. The elevation is approximately the same, but the rainfall is somewhat greater, estimated to be about 35 inches per annum. However, the land is more exposed to strong cold winds. A tract of virgin grass land, typical of the region, was selected for the experiment. This was plowed to a depth of about 16 inches in October. The old grass stools littered the field badly and it required considerable tillage to get the field in planting condition. All plantings were completed within a week after those at Kunia.

The results of the first year's harvest are given in the following table:

Yields of cotton from first year's harvest, Waipahu cooperative experiment.

Plat No.	Variety.	Yield of seed cotton (½ acre).	Yield of lint.	Yield of seed.	Percentage of lint to seed.	Lint calculated to acre yields.
		Pounds.	*Pounds.*	*Pounds.*	*Per cent.*	*Pounds.*
I.	Sea Island, Georgia-Florida strain:					
	Early planting	62½	19½	43¼	31.2	39
	Late planting	42¾	13¼	29½	30.9	26½
II.	Sea Island, "Seabrook":					
	Early planting	277¾	87½	190¼	31	87½
III.	Caravonica "Wool":					
	Early planting	5¼	2.07	3.18	39.4	4.14
	Late planting	[1] 170	[1] 68	[1] 1.02	40	[1] 136
IV.	Egyptian, Mit Afifi:					
	Early planting	146¼	50¾	95½	34.7	101½
	Late planting	23½	8	15½	34.2	16
V.	Upland, "Chinese":					
	Early planting	113	39¼	73¾	34.7	78½
	Late planting	35¼	12¾	22½	36.4	25½

[1] Weight in grams.

A comparison of the Kunia yields with those obtained at Waipahu shows a considerably lower yield for the latter. This can, to only a small degree, be attributed to lack of moisture, because although the soil became quite dry as the season advanced, certain sections in the fertilizer plat gave yields five times as great as the untreated sections under the same condition of moisture. From this it would appear that in these newly opened lands there exists a decided lack of available plant food. The striking differences between the early and late plantings, which were even greater at Waipahu than at Kunia, are largely to be ascribed to a lack of moisture, since at this season no rains occur. From these experiments and the results obtained during the present season, it would seem that early planting is essential on lands in these localities.

The same drawbacks from cutworms experienced at Kunia were repeated here and necessitated the same number of reseedings. It will thus be seen that this pest in itself is an important problem with the cotton grower. The low yields are, of course, in large part to be ascribed to the poor stands and irregular ages of the plants. This is well illustrated by the fact that the yield of 101½ pounds of lint per acre in the case of the early planted Egyptian cotton, represented about 77 per cent of a full stand, without considering the fact that about 60 per cent of the plants represented a second, third, and fourth replanting. It may be further noted that a large number of individual plants from the first sowing averaged 250 bolls per plant, equivalent to at least 2 pounds seed cotton, which would yield approximately 11 ounces of lint. From the above, and from results obtained at the station trial grounds, it would appear that the Egyption cottons have many qualities to recommend them for trial under Hawaiian conditions.

The Caravonica cotton made a much less satisfactory growth at Waipahu than at Kunia, and the yield was nil for all practical purposes. They again started off slowly during the present spring, but as the warm weather came on, appeared to respond quite markedly. However but few bolls have set, and a number of these are falling prematurely, as is also the case on the acre planting made on a neighboring plantation. The cause for this phenomenon has not as yet been determined.

YIELDS.

No data are at hand to show the exact yields obtained from commercial plantings. Reports of yields up to 1,800 pounds of seed cotton per acre for Sea Island and Egyptian cottons have been received from reliable sources, but the areas under consideration have usually been less than an acre. No official report has as yet been made covering the yields of Caravonica cotton from the 25-acre planting at Makaweli, Kauai, but it is understood to have been satisfactory for a first season's crop. The cotton from the private planting of 20 acres at Kunia has not been weighed at this writing, but will probably yield at a somewhat lower rate than on the experimental plat.

Mr. E. C. Smith reports that his 40 plants of Caravonica cotton at the Peninsula, planted in January, 1908, have yielded during the 12 months preceding December 31, 1909, 280 pounds of seed cotton. This would be equivalent to a yield of 4,760 pounds per acre.

Owing to the serious infestation with the bollworm of the cottons grown experimentally at the station grounds, the cultural data of which formed the basis of Press Bulletin No. 24, the second year's yield of merchantable lint was very low.

The yields of all the varieties entering the second year promised an advance over the first year. The Florida and Georgia strains of Sea Island matured their first bolls May 10–25, as against August 8 of the previous year; but the bolls, while of good size and yielding an excellent quality of lint, proved to be infested with the bollworm in very large proportions. This increased as the season advanced and prevented the completion of records of yield for comparison with the first year's crops.

The Caravonica cottons, with the exception of test No. 104, fared similarly. Test No. 104, however, which was located in another field, gave good results both in yield and freedom from pests. The 26 plants in this test were planted in July, 1907. The average yield per plant was 15.2 ounces of seed cotton, as against 6.3 ounces the year previous. The three best selections gave the following yields: Selection 5, 2.43 pounds seed cotton; selection 6, 2.5 pounds seed cotton; selection 9, 3.43 pounds seed cotton.

The main lesson to be learned from this experiment is the seriousness of the pest factor, as has already been pointed out by the station entomologist.

COTTON BREEDING.

During the past year a good foundation has been laid for the cotton breeding work planned a year ago, as announced in Press Bulletin No. 24. During the year an acre planting of the most carefully selected Caravonica seed obtainable and a smaller patch of equally good Sea Island were planted for seed production.

Some 30 standard varieties, represented by the American Upland, Sea Island, Egyptian, and Caravonica types, together with the two wild native cottons, and a Cuban red and a Peruvian tree cotton, were planted in a comparative test. All have done well, and all excepting the last four have completed their first crop. Careful study and copious notes have been made of each variety, and a large num-

PLATE VII.

FIG. 1.—THREE-YEAR-OLD CARAVONICA COTTON TREE BUDDED TO SUPERIOR STRAIN, 3 MONTHS' GROWTH AFTER BUDDING.

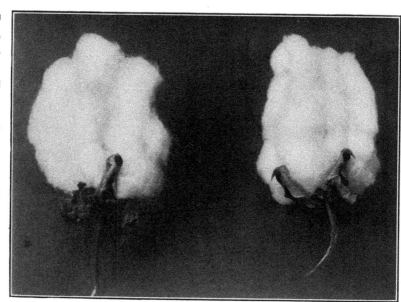

FIG. 2.—IDEAL TYPES OF CARAVONICA "WOOL" COTTON BOLLS.
(Two-thirds natural size.)

FIG. 1.—ONE-YEAR-OLD CUTTINGS OF CARAVONICA COTTON.

FIG. 2.—PLANTS GROWN FROM ABOVE CUTTINGS, 6 MONTHS AFTER TRANSPLANTING.

ber of superior individuals selected as breeding plants. All the inferior plants not destroyed outright have been budded over to the selections. Twelve hundred buds were inserted. Of these, 380, representing 31 per cent, have made satisfactory growth. A large number of cuttings were also made. Of these from 10 to 60 per cent took root. While these percentages are low, the material available was not always good. A number of minor trials under more favorable conditions were very successful, exceeding 80 per cent.

Plate VII, figure 1, shows a 3-year-old Caravonica tree budded over to one of the superior selections shown in figure 2 of the same plate. Eight of the ten buds inserted are making a vigorous growth. Plate VIII, figure 1, illustrates average specimens of the 1-year-old Caravonica cotton cuttings, described in the Annual Report for 1909. In this original experiment, 90 per cent of the Caravonica cuttings rooted. Figure 2 shows the same cuttings six months after transplanting to permanent location. They are making a very vigorous growth and are blooming profusely, a number of the plants averaging a hundred young bolls at this writing.

For the propagation of selections by budding it is now planned to grow seedlings of a vigorous sort in the nursery, as with the common fruits, and when these are from two to three months old to bud low to a single stem. This has already been demonstrated as feasible by Mr. E. C. Smith, a pioneer worker with this method. In Mr. Smith's experiments practically every bud inserted has grown. The day seems near at hand when one may purchase budded seedlings of a pure strain of superior Caravonica cotton by the hundred or thousand. These would be planted out in orchard rows like so many fruit trees, and a full year of cultivation saved, with a possible saving in cost.

MISCELLANEOUS CROPS.

In addition to the comparative tests of rices and cottons, the usual plantings of new crops, to test their adaptability to Hawaiian needs and conditions, have been under trial during the past year. The number of varieties under test during the past spring has exceeded 200. A large proportion of these was personally selected in China and Japan. Among the above a number of sorghums from Africa, and legumes from Japan, give special promise. These will be reported upon in a forthcoming bulletin.

During the year numerous calls were made upon this division for advice pertaining to problems affecting field crops other than rice and cotton. Among these may be mentioned an extensive cropping system involving a 50-acre cooperative experiment, which was planned for the Molokai Ranch Co. This experiment is now well under way, and is showing substantial results.

TARO.

The gradual decline of the taro crop on a 9-acre plantation nea Honolulu has been given some attention during the year. An investi gation of the fields during the height of the harvest season a yea ago showed a deplorable state of affairs. Different patches showe from 20 to 60 per cent of the corms, the edible underground portio of the plant. to be decayed. The decayed portions were returned t the patches "as fertilizer," and in replanting the "hules" from dis eased plants were freely used. No fallowing or rotation had beer practiced for 20 years. Such a practice could not be expected t bring about other results. The general treatment outlined in Bul letin No. 2 of the station, entitled The Root Rot of Taro, by th former agriculturist, was recommended. The results thus far ar very encouraging. Not more than 5 per cent of diseased plants ar apparent at this time, a year after the treatment began.

The agronomist wishes to make acknowledgment of the financia aid and encouragement rendered by a number of the prominent ric growers of the Territory in furthering the rice investigations in China and Japan. Likewise thanks are due to the Japanese and Chinese officials who freely gave information and seeds during th oriental trip. To the members of the station staff who have mad valuable suggestions and rendered material aid in various phases o the work in hand, and especially to my former associates, Messrs Q. Q. Bradford and V. S. Holt, I wish to express my appreciatio for their work on cotton. The former did practically all the budding

A full report of the writer's observations on rice and cotton in vestigations in China and Japan appeared in The Hawaiian Foreste and Agriculturist, beginning with the May, 1910, issue.

○